So That You May Believe

Sermons On The Fourth Gospel

Brand Wesley Eaton

CSS Publishing Company, Inc.
Lima, Ohio

SO THAT YOU MAY BELIEVE
SERMONS ON THE FOURTH GOSPEL

FIRST EDITION
Copyright © 2017
by CSS Publishing Co., Inc.

Library of Congress Cataloging-in-Publication Data

Names: Eaton, Brand Wesley, author.
Title: So that you may believe / Brand Wesley Eaton.
Description: FIRST EDITION. | Lima, Ohio : CSS Publishing Company, Inc., 2017. | Includes bibliographical references and index.
Identifiers: LCCN 2017017141 (print) | LCCN 2017027978 (ebook) | ISBN 9780788029059 (eBook) | ISBN 9780788028427 (pbk. : alk. paper)
Subjects: LCSH: Bible. John--Sermons.
Classification: LCC BS2615.54 (ebook) | LCC BS2615.54 .E28 2017 (print) | DDC
226.5/06--dc23

For more information about CSS Publishing Company resources, visit our website at www.csspub.com, email us at csr@csspub.com, or call (800) 241-4056.

e-book:
ISBN-13: 978-0-7880-2905-9
ISBN-10: 0-7880-2905-3

ISBN-13: 978-0-7880-2842-7
ISBN-10: 0-7880-2842-1   PRINTED IN USA

To my wife, Susan,
who never dreamed she was marrying someone who would
be a preacher when she said, "I do."

Contents

Introduction

As an upstart preacher I had something of an obsession about "discovering my own voice." I believed that if I could develop and settle on a particular method of sermon development and delivery, speaking the word each week as a preaching pastor would eventually become habitual and easy. It would become like parting and combing my hair every morning. After some years, I have come to realize that my development of a particular homiletic method has come to pass, but not in any way or form that I had anticipated. And although it has served me well in pastoral ministry, it has not made preaching habitual or easy. It is nothing like combing my hair every morning.

One of my college majors was archaeology, and my work of biblical interpretation and preaching has borrowed heavily from that discipline. You have certain tools you use and rely upon in an excavation. You have an accepted method for going about the work. However, everything proceeds according to the site itself. The site determines which tools you will use and how you will employ your method. The medium you excavate demands respect. And the medium changes as you go deeper. You encounter different strata of occupation, of living, in the biblical text just as you find different strata of occupation, of history, in excavating an archaeological site. That is especially true, I think, in preaching the gospel of John.

The fourth gospel, with its use of narrative, long discourses, symbolism, and language working at several levels at once challenges the interpreter to proclaim the message of life through belief in Jesus using a multi-vocal approach in the preaching task. Preaching the fourth gospel teaches that "discovering my own voice" means being open to hearing in different ways and speaking in different tones and modalities. The gospel of John opens us to fellowship with Christ at the deepest level of communion by calling to us at different levels, different strata, of our being. So while we are excavating the text, it is, in fact, excavating us.

It is my hope that the following sermons will help readers hear the Fourth Gospel in new ways that lead to transformation, of being excavated personally at a deeper and more profound level of the Spirit. Subsequently, I hope that it will provide readers who preach the Word a cause to stop and reflect upon their interpretive approaches and strategies in working with the biblical texts, and not only the Gospel of John. Perhaps you will find within these pages an impetus for your creative homiletic juices to flow afresh in the sometimes dry and dusty land of weekly sermon preparation and delivery.

I want to thank Frances Taylor Gench, Herbert Worth, and Annie H. Jackson Professor of Biblical Interpretation at Union Presbyterian Seminary. It was through a course in Johannine exegesis taught at Lutheran Theological Seminary at Gettysburg, and taken through the Washington Theological Consortium, while I was an upstart preacher looking for my own voice, that she introduced me to a deeper and transformative reading of the fourth gospel. I also owe an immeasurable debt to the people of York Springs United Methodist Church, who know how to listen well to preaching and respond constructively.

Finally, I want to thank those upon whose shoulders I stand in the ministry of preaching. They are both clergy and laity, some who still walk and work among us and some who have gone on and joined the Church Expectant. I cannot name them all, but God knows them each by name.

BWE
July 2014

John 1:1-5

The Darkness Shall Not Overcome

A sermon in the wake of September 11, 2001

We have gathered today to worship on the Sunday following what is being called the greatest tragedy in our nation's history. We do not yet know how many thousands of our fellow citizens perished in the brutal attacks of this past Tuesday. Many of us have spoken of moving through the days since then as if we have been sleepwalking. The impact that these events shall have on us as a people, and on each of us as individuals, in the coming days is yet to be known. Certainly the world as we have known it is no more, and life for us has been unquestionably altered. On September 11, 2001 darkness fell over the face of the land and the shadows reach long across the days hereafter.

We have no experience in our contemporary memory to compare to these recent events. Nonetheless, we are not strangers to the darkness. We have stories of the darkness that inhabit the deep places of our hearts and minds, so we are not without a reference point in our lives as we seek to face the current darkness that seeks to envelop and swallow us.

We have the story of a child born many years ago to a peasant mother in a client kingdom to the world's greatest empire of that time. She was engaged to be married to a poor artisan; however, she was informed beyond all doubt that the child she was carrying was not his. The situation put her and her child in a very precarious position among her people. For if her intended chose to end the engagement and expose her to the judgment of religious law she could be stoned to death. At best, given that he was known to be a man of righteousness and mercy, he might quietly set her aside to a life of shadowed rejection. But one night during the time in which he was pondering his decision about the matter, in the darkness of sleep, a light shone out to him as an angel in a dream. And the story says that "when Joseph awoke from sleep, he did as the angel of the Lord commanded him; he took her as his wife" (Matthew 1:24).

But the grasping tentacles of the darkness are long, as we know, and relentless. An emperor's decree forced the couple to make a long and arduous trek to the town of their ancestry at the very height of the woman's pregnancy, in order that their names could be registered for taxation. When they arrived at their destination, they found that the darkness had preceded them. No suitable lodging could be found, and the couple was faced with the prospect of not only sleeping outdoors in the cold night, but of perhaps even delivering the child under such conditions of exposure. However, they had kin in the town, and the light shone through those kinfolk in defiance of the plans of darkness. While they had no room to offer the young couple in their household sleeping quarters, they did have room in the household stable among their animals. So the child was born there, and laid in a manger, and the light shined in the darkness.

The darkness was daunted, but not undone, and it hated the light. The light was known now in the world of men, though not yet widely known. And the darkness saw another opportunity to extinguish the light through the jealous and fearful heart of the country's ruler — a man named Herod. The darkness grew in Herod's heart, and it consumed his mind, so that that he saw the tiny light in Bethlehem as a threat. He sent his soldiers to extinguish anyone who might be the light that would threaten the authority of his own kingdom, and other kingdoms, and the kingdom of darkness. But again in his sleep, the light shone out in a dream to the husband of Mary, and he took his family and fled to Egypt beyond the reach of Herod. Nonetheless, the terror of darkness spilled out into the sleepy peace of Bethlehem and robbed the town of its babies. The soldiers of Herod put them to the sword.

Our losses this week were great in number, but no more devastating to us than the killing of their infants was to the mothers of Bethlehem. We, too, now know firsthand the pain of what has been called "the slaughter of the innocents." We have a deeper understanding of that prophecy from Jeremiah, which the storytellers applied to Bethlehem's plight: "A voice was heard in Ramah, wailing and loud lamentation, Rachel weeping for her children; she refused to be consoled, because they are no more" (Matthew 2:18).

How could God let this happen?

Where was the God of love?

Why did so many innocents have to die?

It was impossible in the midst of the darkness for the mothers of Bethlehem to know that the light still shone. In the depth of their grief they could not know that the horrible massacre of their children was not a victory for darkness, but an act of desperation in failure. Yes, the power of darkness had overtaken them, but it could not hold them, for it had not gotten the last word. The light still shone.

And the storytellers tell us the man and woman and the child who fled to Egypt eventually returned, and the child "increased in wisdom and in years, and in divine and human favor" (Luke 2:52). But the darkness never stopped stalking him. For some long time it seemed that the darkness had given up, but all the while it was only waiting for opportunity. As the child became a man who stepped fully into his divine calling, who drew disciples to himself and went into the towns and villages proclaiming the message of God's kingdom and doing what he had come out to do, the darkness mustered itself against him with deeper, ever more malicious intent. Darkness was determined not to fail again.

That the ministry of Jesus drew mounting resistance and opposition from the religious people of his day seems strange and ironic to us. In everything he did, he manifested the reality of God's love and intention of redeeming all creation. Jesus fed the hungry, healed the sick, and ate with sinners, bringing them forgiveness in his name. He is the good news of God. Yet the more his ministry manifested itself, the more the Sadducees and Pharisees and teachers of the Law — the religious people — hated him.

How could it be that deeply religious people, who profess faith in the good and loving God, manifest such scorn and hatred for Jesus as to seek his destruction? Is it that even the most morally upright and devout people are completely rotten at the core of their being? Or could it be that the forces of darkness will use whatever is at hand, twisting and perverting even our virtues and moral convictions to its own ends? Could it be that evil is not something that we harbor so much as it is a force that can overtake us, bringing to pass a level of wickedness in us directly proportionate to our capacity for good? The apostle Paul warns us that "our struggle is not against enemies of blood and flesh, but against the rulers, against the authorities, against the cosmic powers of this present darkness, against the spiritual forces of evil in the heavenly places" (Ephesians 6:12).

It was not so much the leading men and religious authorities among his people who were Jesus' enemies, but it was the forces of darkness, the spiritual forces of evil that used them as instruments for wicked designs. These men, too, were victims of the darkness not much different from the innocent children of Bethlehem. More and more through them the darkness persisted against the goodness of God known in Jesus. But in spite of it all, the light that was in him continued to shine.

As Jesus' life and work pressed on toward their culmination in Jerusalem, the powers of darkness and the spiritual forces of evil gathered their combined strength for an ultimate assault upon the light, the Lord of life. They compounded the jealousies and resentment of an entrenched religious establishment with the fears and anxieties of an occupying imperial power, bringing the full force of iniquity to bear upon him whom we call Savior, Messiah, Christ, and Son of God. And then the unspeakable, the unthinkable, happened.

God made manifest in the flesh submitted himself to the horrible forces of darkness and was swallowed up in a most brutal death. In fear and trembling those who followed him, who loved him and knew him best, deserted him. No angelic-borne message brought saving warning. Death in all its ugliness gathered him in, and with the discordant cackle of ten thousand demons it spiked him to a cross of wood, thrust him through the side, and laid him cold in the ground.

"From noon on, darkness came over the whole land until three in the afternoon. And about three o'clock Jesus cried with a loud voice, 'Eli, Eli, lema sabachthani?' that is, 'My God, my God, who have you forsaken me?'

"Then Jesus cried with a loud voice and breathed his last" (Matthew 27:45-46, 50).

Where was God?

Where was the God of love?

Surely this man was innocent. Why did he have to die?

For three days death's laughter echoed through creation. How could anyone have known that darkness had not really won the victory? How could anyone believe anything other than that death really did give darkness the final word? The best humanity had ever known had brought everything good to bear against its power, only to be swallowed up in death, seemingly never to return. How could we, in the midst of that utter darkness and in the depths of our grief, know that this was not the victory of darkness, but the defining moment of its ultimate failure?

The light disappeared from human sight.

But it did not go out.

Three days after what seemed to be the light's defeat, it rose up from the grave and ascended into an eternal brilliance and glory beyond anything that humanity could have imagined. And in the rising of that resurrected light is the promise that, even though darkness still prowls the earth and the spiritual forces of evil still lurk in heavenly places, their end is being rolled up in the unfolding plan of God revealed in Jesus Christ.

This week, we have been overtaken in the violent death-throes of the world's darkness. We have been sorely stung in a way previously unknown in our experience, and in the midst of our agony the agonized questions of humanity's history have returned.

How could God let this happen?

Where was the God of love?

Why did so many innocent ones have to die?

As those who know in whom our story begins, and who know in whom all human stories find their fulfillment and destiny, perhaps we can begin to realize that these may not be the appropriate questions to ask. As those convinced that we know the end of darkness, while yet recognizing we must still contend with its desperate, futile acts of malice, perhaps we can pose the question that most needs asking and help lead the world to ask it as well.

Is there any word from the Lord? In the midst of this unspeakable, unthinkable tragedy, is there any word from the Lord?

The answer is yes! Yes! The Lord has spoken to the darkness an ultimate word. It is the Word made flesh. What has come into being in him was life, and this life is the light of all people. The light shines in the darkness, and the darkness shall not overcome it.

John 1:19-34

John The Baptizer

A sermon in first-person monologue

I could have found myself some other teacher. There were a number of teachers looking for eager followers. But I went out along the Jordan to listen to this wild man we had heard about, and that was it. I attached myself to John. I'm not really sure why. Maybe it was because he was so radically different from everything and everyone else. Maybe it was his utter disregard of what others thought. Heck, he didn't even try and sell me on becoming his disciple.

"My ministry isn't permanent," he said. "You can stay or go back. Whichever you do, the important thing is you get my message — keep your eyes open for God."

I knew I wasn't going back. I received his baptism and stayed. I thought I understood his message — repentance, the need for radical change. I was sure that staying out in the wilderness as John's disciple was about as radical a change as I could imagine. I later found out that I didn't really understand, at least not yet.

I was there the day the deputation came out from Jerusalem: a bunch of priests and Levites with some Pharisees who had tagged along as observers. They wanted to know who John was. What they were really asking was what or whom he *claimed* to be. He just sort of smirked at them.

"Forget what you're entertaining in your heads," he told them, "I am not the Messiah."

I was half-shocked and half-disappointed to hear John say it. I think all of us, his followers that is, had entertained the notion that John was the promised one. But we had never really brought it up with him, and John had never said anything about it to us. When I heard him so quickly acknowledge to this group of high-hats-and-gowns from Jerusalem that he was not the Messiah, I knew he had been prepared for some time to issue his statement. The interview team wasn't satisfied yet, though.

"Well then, are you Elijah?" they asked.

"Sorry."

"Are you the prophet?"

"Not him, either."

I knew what they were talking about. Hopes for the coming of Messiah had grown during the years what with the way the world was going. People were eagerly expecting the anointed one. But the teachers of the Law had been cautioning everyone that everything would be in accord with the scriptures, and the scriptures indicated that Elijah or the great prophet foretold by Moses (Deuteronomy 8:15) would arise first to prepare the people for the coming of the Day of the Lord. They seemed to have the scenario of Messiah's coming well in hand. All they needed to do was read the signs of the times and put together the pieces from current events. But John wouldn't cooperate, and that sort of aggravated the deputation.

"Well who are you, then? We have to report to the council. What do you have to say for yourself?"

Now as you might expect, John was a bit of a curmudgeon. You know the type. Most of the time they're on the margins of things, not because they just want to be difficult like some folk claim, but because they won't knuckle under to convention. They have the kind of spiritual vision that sees through much of what passes for piety and the courage to call things as they really are. That kind of honesty isn't much welcomed in the mainstream.

Yes, John was a curmudgeon, and he didn't easily or for long entertain fools. So he cut off the questioning very sharply by quoting back a scripture from Isaiah:

"I am the voice of one crying in the wilderness, 'Make straight the way for the Lord.'"

One of the Pharisees saw how this undid the priests and the Levites. He quickly moved the questioning to John's authority for his ministry, asking John why he baptized if he couldn't identify himself as one of their officially acknowledged precursors to the Messiah. But John knew how to change the subject, too.

"I baptize, yes — with water," John replied. "But the real issue isn't me. It's the one who is to come after me. He's among you all right now, but you don't recognize him. If you want to ask about my lack of qualifications, I'm not qualified even to tie his shoes."

At that, the visit was pretty much over.

The next day, still at Bethany on the east bank of the Jordan, John was preaching the reign of God to those who had come out. He was down in the water and was about to make the invitation to baptism when he just stopped. I'd never seen that kind of look in his eyes before. He was looking past us, looking past me, to someone coming toward him off the land.

"The Lamb of God," he said, "there is the one who takes away the world's sin. When I talked about one coming after me who ranks before me, this is he of whom I spoke. Before I was born, he already was. I didn't know who he was, but I know now that this is him. He is why I was sent to baptize, so that he might be revealed to Israel."

I turned then to see. There was quite a crowd, but somehow I knew exactly which man John was talking about. Many of the folk in the crowd didn't seem able to recognize whom John was referring to, but I couldn't mistake him. He wasn't physically remarkable in any way, or of striking appearance. In that way, he was just an average looking guy. Yet, somehow, I knew he was the one. Somehow, I knew there was more to him than what you could see on the surface. While I was looking back at him, I heard John again.

"I saw the Spirit come down from heaven like a dove and come to rest on him. I didn't know him until then. The one who called me to baptize told me that the man on whom I would see the Spirit come down and rest is the one who will baptize in Holy Spirit."

John stepped up from the water toward the man. "I have seen this," he said, "and now I have borne witness — this is the anointed one."

Right then I understood what John meant when he had told me his ministry wasn't permanent. I knew in my soul that there on the river bank near Bethany, John's calling had reached its fulfillment and its peak. I also knew that John had brought me as far along on my journey as he could take me. When I saw in that man on the shore the same thing that John had seen, I was at a crisis point.

Somehow, I knew that I must now leave the one who baptized in water. I had been shown the one who baptizes in the Holy Spirit. Oh, John didn't tell me what I should do. He didn't tell me that I had to move on. He didn't push me to follow the Spirit-baptizer any more than he had tried to make me stay with him at the beginning. He knew you could lead people to water, but you couldn't make them be baptized. He knew, too, that you can show people the living water, but you can't make them drink.

John had done what he had been sent to do: prepare the way and bear witness. He trusted God would take care of the rest.

John 1:35-51

Come And See

Their teacher called the man
By that strange name:
"Lamb of God."
Not knowing what the name meant,
They were drawn to
Follow him.
They were searching for something
That's why they had
Come to John.
John pointed, not to himself,
But to this man
Named Jesus.
You know the eerie feeling —
Being followed
By others.
But he turned to look at them
With peaceful eyes,
Eyes of God.
"What do you look for?" he asked
These two young men,
John's students.
Did his turning frighten them?
Did his speaking
Startle them?
Or was the question he asked
Too close the heart,
Too direct,
Striking their longing that had
First drawn them to
The Baptist?

Was it something in his face?
Perhaps the eyes?
Eyes of God.
It was that which made them follow
That made them call
Him "Rabbi."
It was how they had known John,
These two young men,
John's students.
Now they called Jesus "Rabbi"—
His followers,
His students.
"Where are you staying?" they asked.
But what did they
Want to know?
Was it his address they sought?
The house where he
Lived and slept?
Or was the question deeper
Than they could have
Known themselves?
"Jesus, Rabbi, where are you
From, and where are
You going?"
Did they know? Had they a clue?
Is that what made
Them follow?
Did they guess by where he walked?
Or did they know
From his eyes?
His *question* had been direct,
Touching upon
Their longing.
His *answer* seemed evasive,
Teasing them to
Keep following.

He smiled and said to them, with
Both lips and eyes,
"Come and see."
He did not let them delay.
They must come now
Come and see.

And so they went and stayed with him,
And he with them.
They went to see,
And seeing found they had new eyes.
They saw what had made them follow,
Not just Jesus,
They saw God's Son,
They saw him now through eyes of faith.
In him they saw the Father's love,
The Father's plan.
They saw themselves
No longer longing aimlessly.
With eyes of faith, not eyes of flesh,
They saw their place,
Their destiny.
With Jesus Messiah, Son of Man.
One of the two was named Andrew,
Simon's brother.
He knew his task:
He must tell others, "Come and see."
He went first to brother Simon.
"We have found him:
God's Messiah!
Come, see, and find you have new life."
Simon went to see this Jesus.
He went to see,
He wished to know,
Who it was his brother followed.
Andrew called this man, "Messiah":

God's anointed.
He couldn't be!
Or could he? Simon wished to know.
But Simon had not seen his eyes!
His eyes were deep,
Like cosmic wells.
They saw, not just through space, but time.
Simon went to see and know,
Not to be seen!
Not to be known!
But those eyes could see Simon's soul.
They looked on him before his birth.
They saw his life.
They saw his death.
Those eyes could see the man inside.
And in being known, Simon knew.
In being seen,
Now Simon saw,
With new eyes born from Jesus' heart.
A new name Jesus gave him then.
"You were Simon,
The son of John.
Now you are Cephas, Peter, Rock."

Jesus called Philip: "Follow me."
Philip received
The gift of life
And followed Jesus by faith, not sight.
Like Andrew, Philip knew his task.
He looked up his
Friend Nathanael.
"We have found him, the One foretold."
But Nathanael doubted, and balked.
This one doubted
Before Thomas.
"Can the Prophet come from Nazareth?"

Philip, smiling, said, "Come and see."
Just like Simon,
Nathanael went
And looked into the eyes of God.
Nathanael went to see and know.
He went to find
The One foretold,
And from him received his own soul.

Like them, we are called by others.
We were invited
By brother or friend
To some place Jesus was staying.
We came with curiosity.
We came to see.
We came to know
This One for whom so much was claimed.
Only in our own encounter,
Personally,
With this Jesus
Did we come to know and follow.
In him we know the Father's love,
And we are known.
We have a place:
We're in the Father's family.
Another called us: "Come and see."
But we could not
Know second-hand.
Each must come and meet this Jesus.
This is our task as followers:
To know and to
Be known of him,
And to call others: "Come and see."

John 2:1-11

The Wedding Feast At Cana

Despite the fact that the phrase may be a cliché, many times I've heard the bride at a wedding say to someone, "This is the happiest day of my life." I think many of us, whether married or not, could point to some special day or time in life when it seemed as if everything was bent toward our joy and happiness.

What have been the beautiful moments or principle occasions in your life — this Christmas just past, spent with family and friends; the birth of your own child; a particular victory hard fought for and won; maybe your confirmation into the church, or your baptism into the faith? Perhaps the most significant and joyous event in your life was your wedding day.

Life holds out the promise of many joys, and for many of us the most significant movement of hope and joy is our wedding day. It's the day we celebrate before God and our friends the love we have discovered in our life, and the special bond that we have found with another. Marriage vows are among the most profound vows one can make. No other vows are as tender or more sacred. One opens one's self to the claim of another individual. Two pledge to one another that, while their individual lives remain, they will be lived together as one. But sadly, in too many marriages and in so many other ways in human life, the wine gives out.

Wine, with its sparkle and snap, has long been recognized as a symbol of joy and hope. Folks lift glasses of it in well-wishing and toasting each other at the special times in life. Songs have been written and sung about it. In ancient Israel, wine was a primary ingredient of the wedding feast. Only the chief steward at a wedding would be entrusted with its selection. He tasted it first; he poured it; he directed the serving of it.

At a wedding in Cana of Galilee, Jesus and his disciples were invited guests. While they were in attendance there, a tragedy of sorts began to unfold. At the height of the feast, Jesus' mother comes up to him, telling him that the wine has given out. Perhaps the hosts had ordered too little. Perhaps the guests had drunk too much. Whatever the reason, the wine was gone. The celebration was ending. The party was over.

Life ought to be lived with joy, and the special days of our life ought to be exclamation points of happiness dotting a joy-filled life. But the fabric of our finite lives runs differently than that. The sparkle fades; the joy in life seems to run out, and hope is abbreviated. Christmas, for all the joy and happiness it brings, comes to an end leaving us amidst a pile of unwanted wrapping paper and equally unwanted bills. Dreams evaporate, seemingly before our eyes. Circumstances we had not anticipated enter into our lives, crushing our plans. Marriages fail. Romances cease without ever having reached the altar. Business ventures go sour, leaving us in economic ruin. Factories close down and our job is lost. Working life continues, but our career dies. Loved ones are unexpectedly lost. Our own health is debilitated by accident or disease. The wine gives out.

However, this is only the beginning of the story.

If the only thing this lesson had to tell us is that life and joy run out on us then it wouldn't be worth our time. But there is more to the story, because this is the good news:

Now standing there were six stone water jars for the Jewish rites of purification, each holding twenty or thirty gallons. Jesus said to [the servants], "Fill the jars with water." And they filled them up to the brim. He said to them, "Now draw some out, and take it to the chief steward." So they took it. When the steward tasted the water

that had become wine, [he] called the bridegroom and said to him,
"Everyone serves the good wine first, and then the inferior wine af-
ter the guests have become drunk. But you have kept the good wine
until now" (John 2:6-10).

Every story in the gospel according to John has several meanings running beneath the surface of the story, for
John's gospel is rich in symbolism. There is more to this story, which is our gospel reading for today, than a failed wine
supply at a wedding banquet. When Jesus turned the water into wine, he demonstrated that the future God holds in
store is greater than anything we can conceive. It transcends
our view of the future.

I think the most important thing any of us can do is to
continue looking toward the future with a sense of joyful
expectancy. During their engagement, couples are excited
about planning their future, dreaming about a life together.
In pre-marital counseling, I encourage couples to continue
in their marriage to plan for and dream about the future
together, particularly when facing difficult times. When we
are able to maintain a forward-looking focus in our relationships, we have a broader perspective of life that prevents us
from becoming problem-focused and self-centered. We see
more than ourselves now; we keep a glimpse of what God
is leading us to be.

Something with which my spouse and I struggle, and
that I caution couples about in those pre-marital sessions is
over-reacting when a relationship encounters some rocks in
the road. I believe that we sometimes allow our emotions
to make our problems larger than they really are. We easily can become obsessed with the challenges facing us so
that the challenges are all we begin to see. This is sometimes
also true in our relationships with friends and colleagues at
work. It is very often true in the church, as well. We need to
be cautious not to allow the difficulties we face to set our
agenda.

Jesus never allowed the human predicament to set his agenda. He responded to a larger calling; it was in response to the fulfillment of that calling that Jesus ministered to the need of others. When his mother informs him of the wine shortage at the wedding, Jesus responds in a seemingly rude fashion. "What concern is that to you and me?" he says, "My hour has not yet come." Jesus was not indifferent to need, but neither did he allow the circumstances of individuals to become the focus of his mission. Jesus responded, not out of emptiness, but out of the fullness of God's blessings.

As we face those rocks in the road that challenge the strength of our relationships, we should focus upon our resources — our God-given talents and strengths that we share as a couple, as partners, as friends — for meeting those challenges successfully. Likewise, our congregational life, while responsive to the world's needs, must be grounded in the blessings we enjoy as God's people. We need to be honest with ourselves about our weaknesses, but we need to be realistic about our strength; we do not minister out of human weakness but by the awesome power and grace of God.

We also need to appreciate the everyday and common times in life. Those high points and rites-of-passage in life are certainly important, but they are by far the exceptions. I believe we can find the ordinary to be special when we appreciate our opportunity to share the routine with another, or others.

At the wedding in Cana, the stone jars were common-place things. The water was on hand. Jesus employed both to great advantage. On another occasion, when faced with the need to feed five thousand folks, Jesus made adequate the few fish and loaves that were on hand. When he called apostles to bear the good news, committed orators and theologians were scarce, but eager fishermen and laborers were available. I don't believe our success in living is measured by how good we are at getting the sensational, but how effectively we steward what God has given to us, whether they are on-hand things, or routine time.

I attended the fiftieth anniversary party of a couple who have been long-time family friends. More than one of us there noted the love they could still communicate to one another with just a glance. They were an inspiration to everyone who shared that day with them. That couple was a living image of the hope that is still abroad in our world. But perhaps the thing I will remember most about the anniversary party is the toast that the couple's son offered in their honor. He looked at his mother and father as he raised his glass and said to them, "Mom and Dad, may the best day of your life together past be as the worst day of your life together yet to come."

That is the keystone of the Christian faith. It is the principle that our biblical ancestors and spiritual forebears lived by: thankfulness for life having been lived in communion with God, and the assurance of an even greater future that lay in the hands of God. For them, life today could be lived in joyful confidence because they held to the hope of an even greater life to come.

There is one who has power over the beginning — and ending — of all things, and he has been given the authority to grant new beginnings. Jesus Christ has the power to transform. His is the authority of the light that drives off the darkness. Before him, the ordinary is changed into the glorious; death yields to new life. The water became wine.

In Jesus, God has provided the answer for our most fundamental human yearnings and has shown that, in the providence of God, the best is yet to be. Looking to Jesus, we can be assured that God will meet our needs. We can pledge ourselves to God, opening ourselves to God's claim upon our life, trusting that God will not fail us. When we are in relationship with God, we can have hope for the future. With Jesus Christ, the best is yet to be.

John 3:1-21

Nicodemus

Nick was a bright young man of some promise. He got his bachelor's degree, *summa cum laude*, and then went on for his MBA. After receiving his master's degree, he took a job in the city with First State Bank in their financial services department. First State had recruited him after a summer internship he served with them in the summer after his junior year. They paid for his MBA., brought him on board, and looked forward to his business acumen and personality increasing their investment banking business.

Nick had been at the main office of First State for several years when he began hearing people complain about what was happening up the street. Situated in the city's old commercial district amid Victorian Era financial buildings and stately-but-staid neo-gothic churches, no one at the bank ever imagined such a thing could happen.

"They loiter there on the street sometimes waiting to go in and eat," one of the secretaries said with disgust. "They give me the chills."

"They're a nuisance to people walking through the business district."

"I'm not sure the zoning down here allows that kind of thing."

"Something needs to be done with those people at that church," Nick heard his vice president saying to someone.

Curious about the furor, Nick asked some questions about what was going on. It seemed that one of those old, staid churches had gotten themselves a new pastor — a young woman with progressive social ideas — and she had promptly started a feeding ministry in the church. Unemployed blacks and Hispanics, single mothers, and homeless addicts from the down-at-the-heel neighborhood bordering the commercial district were flooding into the church daily. They were coming for food, both for body and soul — a source of strength for the difficult present and a little hope for the future.

"Why can't they just say their prayers and hold their little services and let things be?" Nick thought to himself. He had been raised in a middle-class home where reward for hard work was the philosophy. His father had always said that most welfare folk were bums who could work, but wouldn't.

"Those people just skim the system," Nick often heard his father say. "Let them sweat for their bread, like I did."

The home where Nick grew up also believed in things "decent and in good order." The thought of dirty street people standing on a corner of the financial district waiting for a handout made him angry.

Eventually some of the corporate entities in the neighborhood filed an injunction to stop the church's feeding ministry. The church filed a counter-motion that the injunction, and the zoning ordinance, on which it was based, violated their religious freedom. The whole mess dragged on for months, and Nick tired of hearing about it. Besides, he had more important things to care about. He had a career to build. There were corporate ladders to climb and money to be made.

"Hard work has its rewards," he kept telling himself. But progress was slow. The financial services market was soft, and gains in sales—and his career—did not come quickly. Nick continued to work late and come in on weekends, pushing himself more and more.

One Saturday morning Nick was in his office crunching numbers, as usual. He was alone in the building, and the work was getting him nothing but a stiff neck. At noontime, he decided to take a walk. His jaunt took him unknowingly past the church with the soup kitchen. He didn't see any crowd milling about outside, and he assumed that the church's feeding ministry kept bankers' hours.

"They probably do it just to attract attention," he told himself. But as he passed the stairs leading down to the church's lower level, he heard the sound of singing.

> *I surrender all,*
>> *I surrender all,*
>>> *All to Jesus I surrender,*
>>>> *I surrender all.*

Somehow the sheer absurdity of those words, sung by people who needed free victuals, drew him in. He slipped quietly down the stairs and through a door into a brightly lit hall filled with tables and chairs, where a number of shabbily dressed and ungroomed men and women sat with trays containing dirty utensils and spent napkins. At the front was a young woman in jeans and a sweatshirt. The singing had stopped, and she was reading from a Bible.

"In very truth I tell you, no one can see the kingdom of God unless he has been born again."

Nick thought it interesting to hear Jesus speak with a woman's voice.

"The wind blows where it wills; you hear the sound of it, but you do not know where it comes from or where it is going. So it is with everyone who is born from the Spirit."

The woman looked up from her Bible and looked right at him. He thought of going right back out the door, but her gaze held him. Without surrendering eye contact, she crossed the room to where he was standing.

"We never have visitors such as you," she said to Nick. "Can I help you?"

"No, no. I'm sure I don't need anything," Nick replied, half-embarrassed. "I was just happening by and I heard the singing. I was curious about the source of so much fuss among your neighbors."

"I think you must be some of those neighbors," she replied.

"I'm surprised that you would want to be seen here."

"I'm surprised to hear you reading the born-again thing," he retorted. "I thought that was just for TV evangelists."

She came back at him quickly. "Perhaps you shouldn't base your understanding of Christianity on TV evangelists — or the opinions of the downtown banking establishment. Being born again isn't what you may think."

"I'm not completely ignorant," Nick snapped. "I had a few religion courses in college. Wasn't Jesus speaking about something spiritual when he talked about being 'born again'? What's spiritual about all of this? Seems to me if that's your focus you ought to be organizing prayer meetings, not spooning soup to junkies."

"You know," she said to him, now in a softer tone, "I think if you really believed that, you would have never come down those stairs."

His eyes narrowed. The very suggestion caught him by surprise, but somehow only at a superficial level. Why had he come down the stairs? Was it morbid curiosity — a desire to see how "the other half" lived? Was it the bizarre words of that hymn he had heard them singing? Or was this woman church leader right? Was it something inside him that had drawn him downstairs to the soup kitchen? Was there some kind of gap between what he had learned and what he knew to be true? Was it some kind of nagging dissonance somewhere inside him that had brought him into the church basement?

He turned and walked out without saying more, but the encounter stayed with him all that week. Every night on leaving the office, he stopped to look down the street toward the church —toward the place where he had heard hungry street people singing.

I surrender all,
   I surrender all,
      All to Jesus I surrender,
        I surrender all.

The next Saturday at noontime, when there was no one else in the office to know where he was going, he went back down to the church soup kitchen. And he went down again the Saturday after that. He sat down in the back and watched them eat and listened to them sing. One bearded old man in a knit beanie got up during the singing and came back to where Nick was sitting. When Nick looked up at him, the old man put an apple on the table.

"Here," the old man said, without expression. "They always give us fruit, but I hain't got teeth for apples," he said. "You kin go up and git soup an' a san'wich if you're really hungry," he offered.

Nick looked up into the old man's face. It was worn and tired, but Nick saw life in the eyes — life like he had never seen before. He smiled without words and took the apple. He walked up to the serving window, but not for food. Pastor Sally was there, reading again from John's gospel.

"It was not to judge the world that God sent his Son into the world," she continued to read as she watched Nick approach, "but that through him the world might be saved."

"Can I ask you something?" he said to her.

That Wednesday at noon, Nick did something very out of character. Instead of working through lunch, he grabbed his coat and started out of the office.

"Wow! You going out for lunch today, Nick?" someone asked him on his way to the door.

"Sort of. I'm going up the street to help serve it," Nick replied flatly. He wasn't completely comfortable with what he was doing. He worried somewhat about how this was all going to sit with the bank. But he would have to deal with it. What he had seen in the old man's eyes that past Saturday was bigger than the bank, bigger than his career, or any number of careers. It had washed out all of the easy, but false, black-and-white views he had been living by. Perhaps he had caught a glimmer of what being 'born again' was all about. And for Nick, it meant that life was never going to be quite so simple ever again.

John 4:46-54

The Royal Official's Son

The father realized that this was the hour when Jesus had said to him, "Your son will live." So he himself believed, along with his whole household (John 4: 53).

Prayer:
Loving God, may your word proclaimed and received in the power of your Holy Spirit evoke belief in those in whom it is lacking, strengthen it in those whom it is weak, and bring new life in those whom it is growing; through Jesus Christ our Lord. Amen.

The gospel according to John opens by telling its readers that God came in the person of Jesus Christ, so that all who receive him and believe in his name might become children of God (cf.: John 1:12). The evangelist may have originally concluded his gospel at the end of chapter twenty by stating that he has written "so that you may come to believe that Jesus is the Messiah, the Son of God, and that through believing you may have life in his name" (John 20:30). From beginning to ending, the theme of the gospel is belief in Jesus.

But what does it mean to believe? What do we need to believe in order to have life in the name of Jesus? What is the belief that gives us power to become "children of God?" Many of the Judean Jews and the Galileans in John's gospel demonstrate a certain belief in the name of Jesus because of the signs he performed. However, it is not these who demonstrate the saving belief of which the gospel speaks. It is rather the belief of the royal official, who seeks Jesus out in order that Jesus may heal his son, who demonstrates the kind of belief that leads to life.

So that we might also know the belief that leads to life, we need to first carefully note the particulars of this story of the royal official who seeks out Jesus. Secondly, I propose that we compare his belief with that demonstrated by the generality of people who encountered Jesus. I will then conclude with a few brief reflections on contemporary patterns of belief.

I.

First, let's begin by taking an in-depth look at this gospel story. Jesus came to Cana, where, as the evangelist recalls, he performed his first sign of changing water into wine at a wedding. A royal official, attached to the court of Herod Antipas at Capernaum, had a desperately ill child. He heard that Jesus was back in the area, and he made the eighteen-mile trip from Capernaum to Cana to seek an audience with Jesus. We don't know if this man had heard about the signs Jesus performed while at the Passover celebration in Jerusalem, or if he had heard about the miracle of the wine at the wedding. Whatever led him to know anything about Jesus, he believed Jesus was able to heal his son, and he begged him to come to Capernaum.

At first reading, it may seem that Jesus rebuked the man as a superficial seeker after the miraculous. However, when Jesus said, "Unless *you* see signs and wonders you will not believe" (John 4:48), the word the Evangelist uses for "you" is plural. Therefore, it seems that Jesus was not addressing the official so much as he was speaking to some unspecified bystanders. At any rate, the grave condition of the official's son would not allow him to stand about and tolerate time spent on a sermon concerning the appropriate basis of belief (such as all of you are doing right now!). The man said to

Jesus, very directly, "Sir, come down before my little boy dies" (John 4:49).

There may be no words spoken anywhere in the Bible more poignant than this point-blank plea from the royal official. However Jesus did not actually honor the man's command. Instead, he issued one of his own: "Go, your son will live" (John 4:50).

I recall telephoning the doctor's office on more than one occasion when one of our children was ill. I can remember the sense of relief I felt from hearing the receptionist tell me that the doctor was advising that I bring my child in to the office to be seen. I felt the doctor could then make a first-hand assessment of my child's condition, and begin the appropriate treatment immediately. Being asked to come in and spend fifty, seventy-five, or a hundred dollars somehow gave me peace of mind!

Jesus did not agree to go down to Capernaum and see the official's son. He flatly told the man to go on his way home; the child would be made well without the house call.

Amazingly, the official complied with Jesus' command. He did not question the veracity of Jesus' promise, but "believed the word Jesus spoke to him and started on his way" (John 4:50). Here we glimpse a profound transition in the faith journey of an individual.

When I was a very young man, apprenticing in the electrical trades, I worked under a journeyman electrician who was very good in his field. Working side by side with him, I was always confident of what I was doing. But there were times when we would be working a large job, and he would send me off to do some part of the work on my own with his instructions, in order to accomplish more of the task. Separated from him, my confidence in my knowledge and ability faded. I also often found myself doubting the instructions I had been given. My journeyman overseer wasn't right there to see what was really needed. What if he was wrong?

It is a big spiritual step to go from having trust in someone while in their physical presence to trusting their word
after being separated from them by some time and some distance. The royal official with a desperately ill child demonstrates a trusting belief in the word of Jesus apart from his
physical presence.

As the man made his way to Capernaum, he was greet-
ed on the second day of his return trip by some of his own
servants. They joyfully told him that his son had recovered.
When he asked them when the boy's recovery began, they
told him a time the previous day that coincided with the
time when Jesus told him his son would live. The fulfillment of Jesus' word evokes yet another level of belief in the
father. The evangelist said that upon hearing the news the
man "himself believed, along with his whole household"
(John 4:53). This believing comes not only to the royal official, but also to everyone in his house. It is the climax of
a faith journey that begins with *belief in words about Jesus*,
grows to a *trust in the words of Jesus*, and finds fulfillment in
belief in the person of Jesus himself.

II.

Secondly, I proposed to compare how the belief of the
royal official differs from the faith of many of the other people whom Jesus encounters. From what we read in the gospel according to John, belief in Jesus begins with the signs
that Jesus performed. When Jesus changed the water into
wine at the Cana wedding, John writes that, subsequently "his disciples believed in him" (John 2:12). When Jesus
cleansed the temple at Jerusalem, and performed other un-
told signs at the Passover festival, "many believed in his
name because they saw the signs that he was doing" (John
2:23). When Jesus fed a multitude with five barley loaves
and a couple of fish, the people "saw the sign that he had
done, [and] began to say, 'This is indeed the prophet who is
to come into the world'" (John 6:14).

The belief of the royal official, unlike the kind of belief demonstrated by many others who had witnessed or heard about Jesus' miraculous signs, continues to grow. While others are content with the benefit of the signs alone, this man moves toward a deeper personal encounter with Jesus. While some who believed in Jesus because of the signs eventually rejected his words, the royal official — even at the risk of his son's life — comes to take Jesus at his word. In finding Jesus' word fulfilled in the restoration of his son's life, the royal official gains something he had not counted on: faith leading to new life for himself and his whole household.

Which level of the royal official's belief, what degree of his faith, brought him to this new life? Every level! Every degree of his faith — even the belief based upon what he had heard *about* Jesus' signs — was saving faith. You see it isn't the *degree* of faith demonstrated that was significant, but the *kind* of faith. Even when the royal official's belief was not one degree above that of most other people who had seen or heard about Jesus, it differed from theirs in kind. For he had the kind of faith, of belief, that seeks always to go on to the next level of relationship with the object of belief.

III.

Understanding the significant difference in belief to be a difference of kind rather than degree ought to be a matter of some pause to us. I believe you can discern three kinds of belief among those who commonly call themselves Christians.

Some have a belief comparable to that held by those who acknowledged the benefit of Jesus' miraculous signs but who sought to go no further with him. You believe religion is a good thing for teaching children proper moral values, for providing the dominant culture with a sense of decency, and for maintaining a stable society. You have a certain respect for the work the church does in helping folks out, and you are even willing to contribute something toward that work yourself. You don't mind attending worship whenever some other activity doesn't prevent you, and you're able to recite the Apostles' Creed just fine without any reservation of conscience. Jesus Christ has a place in your life — albeit alongside other significant things, such as your patriotic devotion to country, your commitment to your job, and the enjoyment of your hobbies. However you haven't any intention of ever allowing Christ a place of prominence in your life. You are thankful for the benefit you believe you receive from his signs, so long as the status quo is maintained. Many of us start at just such a level of belief, but the kind of belief that refuses to go beyond this is hardly any belief at all. The demons of hell have that much belief. They, too, can recite the Apostles' Creed, so long as the Christ it confesses doesn't interfere with the world's current perverse arrangements, and their own success in that context. This kind of belief will make you a fine friend of the world, but not a child of God.

Some profess a belief that admits to the need of obeying Christ's commands. You have the kind of faith based upon religious authority. Many of you make excellent church people. You are supportive of the church in that it gives your world structure and order. You appreciate doing things right, according to all the rules. You have the kind of faith demonstrated by many of the Pharisees of Jesus' time — a willingness to obey the ordinances of God, as long as God keeps at a safe distance. Your belief allows for God to be easily codified into a system of dos-and-don'ts. God's word can be neatly followed, and Jesus Christ can be relied upon not to cause you any upset. However, your faith precludes a real love relationship with Christ. A love relationship might issue in complications to your sense of propriety, or a radical shift in your understanding of yourself. Jesus spoke about your kind of faith when he said that someday many would say to him, "Lord, Lord did we not do many deeds of power in your name?" to whom he will declare, "Go away; I never knew you" (cf. Mt. 7:22-23).

But, thanks be to God, there are those whose belief constantly seeks a deeper understanding and a greater relationship with the believed. It is a belief that seeks to trust as a child trusts in a loving parent. Your obedience is born of love rather than a compelling need for order. You long for openness to the will of God that goes beyond mere acceptance to a yearning desire. Your recitation of the Creed is like the repetition of wedding vows. You strive to know more of, not merely more about, the one who gives life. You give Christ the preeminence, even though it costs you personally. You know the pain of Christ complicating your life, and you know the joy of following him unconditionally.

Whatever *degree* of belief you know in yourself today, of what *kind* is it? Can you profess a desire for more of Jesus Christ? Do you have that heartfelt assurance that you are a child of God? Are you yearning after the one who can grant it? Your faith may have its beginning in no more than a sign, but the belief leading to eternal life finds its completion in Jesus Christ. May you come to believe in Jesus the Messiah, the Son of God, and through believing may you have life in his name.

John 5:1-18

Do You Want To Be Made Well?

"Jesus the healer" may be the most common New Testament image of the Lord. Throughout the gospels, we read stories of Jesus performing miraculous healings. However, the story of Jesus healing the man at the pool of Bethzatha is unique.

When a paralytic is let down on a litter through the roof of a house where Jesus is teaching, he says to the paralytic, "Your sins are forgiven" (Matthew 9:2, Mark 2:5, Luke 5:20). When a woman with a chronic hemorrhage touches Jesus' clothes in a crowd and is healed, Jesus tells her, "Daughter, your faith has made you well" (Mark 5:34, Luke 8:48). When a centurion comes to Jesus seeking the healing of his servant, Jesus commends this Gentile for having faith greater than many in Israel (Matthew 8:10, Luke 7:9).

The story of the man at the pool of Bethzatha is different. There is no pleading request for healing from the man, nor does Jesus offer any commendation of the man's faith. It is Jesus who takes the initiative in this healing, approaching the one who is sick with a very direct question: "Do you want to be made well?" (John 5:6). However, the man's response is not direct. In fact, he avoids answering and instead offers an excuse: "Sir, I have no one to put me into the pool when the water is stirred up; and while I am making my way, someone else steps down ahead of me" (John 5:7).

It seems that at certain times, the water of this colonnaded pool would become agitated. It was believed that an angel stirred the water, and whoever entered the pool first at such times received healing of whatever disease. Rather than tell Jesus that he wanted to be healed, this man was more intent on explaining why he had remained sick for so long. Undistracted by the man's answer, Jesus spoke to him a simple command: "Stand up, take your mat and walk" (John 5:8). And at once the man was made well.

I wonder: is that what the man really wanted? I wonder if he was not more content to remain ill. He isn't well very long before his life is complicated greatly because of his healing. He does not go far carrying his mat before being confronted by some of the religious leaders, who take exception with what he is doing. Carrying any burden on the sabbath was considered sabbath-breaking, and they tell the man he is sinning by carrying his mat. Better at excuses than explanations, the man's defense is that his healer instructed him to take up his mat and walk. But this only leads to further interrogation by the religious leaders.

"Who is the man who said to you, 'Take it up and walk'?" they asked (John 5:12). But he was unable to give a satisfactory answer, for Jesus had disappeared into the crowd before the man could identify him. Later, Jesus encountered the man in the Temple and warns him to give up his sinful ways, so that nothing worse may befall him. The man's ungrateful response is repugnant. He went straightway and identified Jesus to the religious leaders, who began persecuting him as a sabbath breaker.

The story of the man who Jesus healed at the pool of Bethzatha was different from others of Jesus' healings that the gospels relate, but the man's response to Jesus' initial query was perhaps not all that unusual.

> "Do you want to be made well?"
> "I'd like to get back to working and doing things, Lord, but I don't think I could afford it."
> "Do you want to be made well?
> "Lord, I just can't get comfortable being out in public since my spouse died."
> "Do you want to be made well?"
> "Lord, every time I've tried to reconcile with her, she just says something that starts the whole argument over again."

Perhaps the other stories of Jesus healing are the exceptional stories. Perhaps the man at the pool of Bethzatha and his reaction to Jesus' offer of healing are not the exception, but the rule. We resist being made well, because it is easier for us to remain sick, to remain a victim. To be made well emotionally may mean being made able to contribute. To be made well physically may mean being made responsible. To be made well in our relationships may mean the hard work of beginning again with one from whom we have been estranged. To be made well by Jesus means being made whole and given a new life. Are we too comfortable with our brokenness and death?

God's desire is redemption — wholeness for a broken creation. God intends to bring that wholeness begun in Jesus to completion. God's desire for each of us is wholeness, healing, and newness of life. But, when we are honest with ourselves, we know that God's promise is both joyful and frightening for us. For we have learned to get on with a reduced life, with our brokenness, and being healed and made whole in Christ will mean making a commitment to living a life of wholeness. It may mean accepting complications, encountering further conflict, being responsible, perhaps loving someone who is more easily despised. Being healed and made whole, means sharing in the life we find in Jesus.

Do you want to be made well?

John 6:1-21

The Miracle Of The Loaves

We talked about going down to Jerusalem for the Passover. Everyone was always moved by the services at the temple and the solemnity of the Feast. But Jesus seemed disinterested in going to the Holy City this year.

"I have a better idea," he said. "Let me take you on retreat, and I will show you the glory of God."

Intrigued by his invitation, we all quickly consented. Besides, getting away together with Jesus sounded better than fighting the Passover crowds in Jerusalem. We hired a boat and rowed across Galilee to the Golan Heights — the perfect site for a spring retreat.

We landed and went straight up the Heights on to a grassy knoll that Jesus seemed already to know about. It was a beautiful place with a commanding view all around. Two or three boys from a nearby village were there on the hillside jumping frogs. Some of the group stopped to talk with them, while Jesus and the rest of us found a nice place to sit down overlooking the north shore of the Sea.

We were sitting there, just kind of quietly soaking up the gentle sun. I was leaning back on my arms, my face tilted toward the sun with my eyes closed. I was thinking about how great a Passover this was going to be. Here we were, on retreat with the Master, and he had promised to reveal to us the glory of God.

Just then one of the others sitting there nudged me. I opened one eye to look at him, but he was pointing down the hillside, wide-eyed.

"Look at all of them, will you!" he said.

I sat up and peered down the hill, my eyes taking a bit to adjust to the light. I couldn't believe what I saw. There must have been five thousand or more of them gathering on the hillside, pointing up at us, and calling out to Jesus, "Rabbi! Rabbi!"

"Isn't this great?" I said sarcastically to myself. So much for being on retreat — just us and Jesus and the glory of God. I might as well have gone to Jerusalem.

We all stood up to look at the crowd. Those who had stopped to talk with the young boys from the village noticed and came over with us. James let his breath go between his teeth in a sort of whistling sound when he saw all the people.

"Whew-ee! Would you look at all of 'em?"

While still looking down at the crowd, Jesus said to Philip, "Where will we buy bread for all these folk?"

Philip looked at Jesus incredulously. "A half-year's salary wouldn't buy enough for each of them to get even a crumb!" he exclaimed.

But Jesus just looked at Andrew and smiled. It was a smile that indicated he knew something no one else knew. Andrew looked back at Jesus anxiously, and then he blurted out, almost as if embarrassed, "One of the boys has a couple of fish and a few barley loaves. But just our group couldn't make lunch out of that." Jesus responded by sending us to go have the people sit while he had Andrew introduce him to his young lunch-packing friend.

"Well, this is certainly under-whelming," I thought to myself as I went through the crowd motioning for them to sit down. They were a motley bunch — farmers, fishermen, shepherds, and day laborers. Nothing in that crowd looked faintly glorious, even by human standards. Unless Jesus was going to turn them into something else, like he did with the water at that wedding, this holiday was wasted.

We got them all seated and rejoined Jesus, who was taking the kid's lunch out of the sack. Then he held the fish and rough barley bread in his hands and offered thanks. I never felt so stupid and embarrassed in my whole life. I wondered what manner of hate and discontent would break out in the crowd when the first ten people got food and everyone else went without.

After the blessing, Jesus handed out the bread and fish. I stood and watched while a lump formed in my throat. But something strange happened. Twenty or thirty people had received, and they were still passing on food! A quarter of the crowd, then perhaps half of them, was eating, and still they were passing food! I stood for a while in amazement as the whole crowd took food. Then I plopped down in the grass next to Jesus, who was intently watching the impromptu banquet take place.

After a while, Jesus spoke up again. "Gentlemen," he said to us, "there are leftovers I'd like you to retrieve. We don't want to waste anything, and you all need to eat, too."

We picked up twelve baskets of leftover fillets and barley bread! "Twelve," I thought, "as in twelve tribes of Israel." I looked up at Jesus as I came back toward him from the crowd. He was smiling that too-knowing smile again. Before I reached him, my attention was drawn back to the crowd.

It started as a murmur and proceeded to become almost a chorus. "Messiah!" you could hear people saying. "The prophet! Let him be our king, our redeemer from the Romans!"

"This is it!" I thought. Here was the glory Jesus promised to reveal to us! Jesus knew what was going on all the time. He had brought us out to see him popularly proclaimed king of Israel. With the crowd he had drawn out here in the boondocks, why, in no time he would be leading a conquering army into Jerusalem. This really was a revelation of glory! I turned and began running up the hill. I wanted to grab the master and hug him, and shout out in praise. But when I reached the knoll, I couldn't find him. The crowd, too, was anxiously looking for him, but he was nowhere to be found. Then I heard Simon Peter.

"I don't get it," he was saying. "As soon as he heard all this stuff about messiah and king and beating the Romans, he went off into the hills by himself."

We waited about there until the latter part of the evening, but Jesus did not come back down.

"We might as well row back to Capernaum," James suggested. We got into the boat, pushed off, and each of us grabbed an oar. As I pulled hard through the water, I looked back at the crowd on the beach, watching us leave. I thought about the events of the day. It was to have been a retreat, a time apart when we could learn deeply from the master. He had promised us a glimpse of God's glory. But these people, these farmers and shepherds, had shown up. And Jesus fed them to satisfaction with practically nothing. Then just when I thought God's will might be revealed through Jesus in all its might and fullness, he was gone. He ran away from being king. He ran up into the hills and left us there with that riff-raff.

The rowing was hard. The wind was up and the sea was rough. It was that in-between time when it is almost dark. I wouldn't say any of us were really scared, but we were working hard against the sea. And we were confused.

Suddenly, several of the company let out a yell. Everyone froze paralyzed at their oar and looked over the stern in stark terror at a figure walking on the surface of the water toward us! I don't know who was sitting behind me, but I heard him catch his breath and squeak out in a terrified whisper, "Glory be!"

I could see then that the figure on the water was Jesus.

"I am," he said, "do not fear."

Then it struck me. "Yes, 'I Am.' I Am who I Am. Just as you revealed yourself to Moses from a bush, so today you revealed yourself to us as the gracious host of a feast. I Am will be the gracious host of the heavenly banquet."

Just then we hit the shore at Capernaum.
"I Am," I said to myself again.
Glory be, indeed.

John 6:53-59

The Living Bread

Today we come to the table of the Lord: Holy Communion. As one called to a ministry of word, order, sacrament, and service, it is my duty and privilege to preside at the table. For me, this is one of the most enjoyable and uplifting parts of pastoral ministry. However, I also am charged with teaching what our church believes about the meaning and significance of Holy Communion. That's something more of a challenge.

Why do we share in this sacred meal? How are we spiritually fed in receiving these common elements of bread and wine? When we talk of these things being "the body and blood of Christ," are we just making word pictures? What kind of reality are we talking about in using these words?

I think flesh and blood is the best place I can start. Jesus said, "Unless you eat the flesh of the Son of Man and drink his blood, you have no life in you" (John 6:53). If I say to you that I am here today in the flesh, you know what I'm talking about. There is meaningfulness about my talking to in the flesh that cannot be attained by my talking to you in any other way.

A few years ago, in a denominational magazine published for clergy, I read an article about the growing use of electronic media in worship. One of the ideas put forth in the article was the churches could network via satellite hook-ups and broadcast sermons on Sunday mornings from mega-churches whose preachers are the leading pulpit voices in the country. The author of this idea supported it by saying that, in this way, every congregation could be assured of high quality preaching every week. You could be treated to the preaching of those who minister in some of the world's largest and fastest growing churches.

Personally, I don't believe the author of the article knew that much about preaching. Preaching is not a one-way event. It is not simply about the content of a sermon. It also is about the energy that flows in the sermon from preacher to congregation and back again. The proclamation of the Word is a two-way event and it is an incarnational event—that is, it happens in the flesh. What kind of a witness does a cyber-sermon make for a faith that believes in the Incarnation?

In the early days of Christianity, one of the great struggles of belief concerned people who said that Christ did not really come in the flesh, but that he only appeared to be human. After all, they argued, the ineffable, unchanging God would never demean himself to take on real human existence. These people came to be known as Docetists, after the Greek word that means "to seem," since they professed that Christ only seemed to be human. Such a Christ seems to be about as one-dimensional as a big-screen preacher. There is meaningfulness to knowing Christ in the flesh.

At the table of the Lord, as we partake of the common bread and wine, we profess that Christ has come in the flesh, and is no less present with us at the table than he was present at the table in the upper room with his first disciples. Certainly we profess that Christ is always present in the Holy Spirit with us, but in Holy Communion we experience the reality of Christ's presence with us in a unique way. I cannot explain it scientifically, nor prove it empirically, and back it all up with data. I can only explain it spiritually, tell you his flesh and blood presence at the table in receiving the bread and the wine is known by faith.

Secondly, Jesus said, "Those who eat my flesh and drink my blood abide in me, and I in them" (John 6:56). He speaks of an interrelationship with us in Holy Communion that dares human language to explain. The best that I can do is to give you an illustration by which you may glimpse the depth of this interrelationship we are offered in Christ.

Yesterday, I officiated at a wedding. In the traditional United Methodist wedding liturgy, the ceremony begins with this greeting:

> *Dearly beloved, we are gathered together here in the sight of God, and in the presence of these witnesses, to join together this man and this woman in holy matrimony, which is an honorable estate, instituted of God, and signifying unto us the mystical union that exists between Christ and his Church.*[1]

Marriage signifies to us the mystical union that exists between Christ and his church. The Passover was regarded as God's marriage to his people long before Jesus was born. Much of what Jesus did at the Last Supper, in fact, resembled the actions of a Jewish wedding of the time.

In a Jewish wedding the bridegroom sought first to bring the bride to his home. Jesus invited the disciples to supper in the room lent to him, since he had no home. When the bridegroom got the bride home, he first of all knelt and washed her feet. Jesus washed the disciples' feet. Then at a Jewish wedding the wedding feast followed. Jesus ate roast lamb and unleavened bread with his disciples. After supper at a Jewish wedding came the words of the wedding covenant. Jesus made a new covenant with symbols of broken bread and poured out wine.

Now, if someone can deliver a completely satisfying explanation of the depth of union and interrelationship found in a marriage between two people who deeply love each other, I welcome them to try. We can *know* that relationship by personal experience, but a satisfactory explanation eludes us. We can talk about the love of the marriage relationship, the desire of physical intimacy with the person we love, the warmth of being together. But these expressions

1 From page 93 The United Methodist Book of Worship

cannot fully communicate that sense of united being, which we have with a loved and loving marriage partner.

To lift up marriage as an illustration is to necessarily say that the depth of communion we experience in marriage is *close* to the relationship we are offered with Christ in Holy Communion. We abide with him and he abides with us. Beyond Jesus' own words, I'm not sure much better explanation can be offered.

Thirdly, Jesus said, "Just as the living Father sent me, and I live because of the Father, so whoever eats me will live because of me" (John 6:57). Jesus Christ brings us into relationship with himself at the table, and with God the Father.

The Scriptures talk about the resurrected Christ interceding with the Father on our behalf. When I read Scripture my mind works in pictures. What I do not picture is Christ abjectly pleading before God the Father, that he may have mercy upon his own children. I see Christ at work with us and within us, by all the ways open to love — without coercion or bribing — to affect a unity, a full "at-one-ment" between us and God. He is acting on behalf of us because he has committed himself to us. He who has one hand in the hand of God the Father has his other hand in our hand. And his own hands only come together as he puts our hand into the Father's hand. And he will have completed his work only when we are completely one with God. He does that in his body, where the fullness of humanity and the fullness of God meet, become at one, and enter into mystical union. He offers us that opportunity by coming among us in the flesh. He is *Living Bread*.

John 7:37-52

The Unbelief Of Those In Authority

Jane dropped the folder on the passenger seat as she slid behind the wheel of her car. She would miss being with her classmates during the break, but she was glad the semester was over. The car turned over slowly at first, and then fired. "Thank you, Lord," Jane prayed without words. She would have to have the battery replaced when she got home. Right now, she was just grateful that a weak car battery wasn't going to make her miss the interview.

At the first traffic light on the way out of town, Jane opened the folder on the seat next to her as she waited for the light to change. Inside was a copy of her application material to the Committee on Ministry. She was hopeful but anxious about the interview with the Committee. Getting them to accept her as a candidate for ordination had been something of a struggle. They had been reticent to believe that, at eighteen years old, she could really know that she had an authentic call to be a pastor. She had sat in the hallway outside the meeting room much longer than was comfortable, and when they had called her back in she was sure they were going to send her home with advice to ponder what she was feeling and perhaps come back in a year. Instead, she was accepted as a candidate by a split vote of the committee.

Now she was 21, a senior in college, and she had applied to have her candidacy certified. This certification approval by the Committee on Ministry would qualify her for grant money from the denomination for her studies. It would also permit her to apply for a license to preach. The license would give her authority to provide pastoral supply and gain some real experience in the pulpit. All of that hinged on the interview with the nine members of the Committee on Ministry. She was glad it had been arranged for her to meet with them on the drive home for semester break. After the interview, she could drive home where her support network in her local church would offer celebration or solace.

Jane arrived on time for her interview, but the Committee on Ministry was running a little behind on its schedule, and she was one of four candidates being interviewed that day. As Jane waited her turn to meet the committee, she reflected on her journey thus far. She had loved Sunday school as a child, especially the stories about the women of the Bible. She thought about the story of Deborah the judge of Israel and how the general of Israel's armies, Barak, would not engage the Canaanites under Sisera unless Deborah would accompany him. She loved the story of Deborah, because the Bible called her a prophet and she held a place of leadership because God's Spirit was with her.

She thought about her participation in youth ministry. She was very active with the conference youth group, actively participating in planning meetings and conference youth missions. A sense of resentment came over her as she remembered how she had once been nominated for president of the conference youth fellowship. She had lost that election to a boy who, although not as active in the ministry, came from one of the conference's city churches. Jane's identity as a female, and a female from a rural congregation, had often worked against her in conference-wide activities.

Her feelings of resentment quickly dissipated when the door to the meeting room came open, and Jane was called inside. She was introduced to the current members of the committee — some of whom she had met before and others she did not know. After the introductions and an opening time of prayer, the chairperson stated again the purpose of the meeting with Jane. Her record as an exploring candidate for ministry during the previous three years was reviewed. It was shared that she was now a senior at a church-related college, majoring in religion. She was coming before the committee today, having applied for certification of her ministerial candidacy. At that point, the chairperson asked Jane if she wished to address the committee.

Jane talked briefly about feeling very close to God from her childhood. She talked about her growing up in a small rural church, of becoming involved in conference youth work, the summers spent during college counseling at church camp, and the growing sense throughout her brief life that she was called to be a pastor of God's people. After she finished speaking, the chairperson invited questions from committee members.

What some of the committee members asked Jane stunned her. She expected to be questioned about her sense of the church's mission, the gifts and graces needed for pastoral ministry, and something about her knowledge of the church's doctrine. While one or two questions grazed those subjects, most of what she was asked seemed irrelevant to her.

What extra-curricular activities had she been engaged in during her college years? Where had she worshiped while she was away from home? Had she experienced worship and fellowship in any of the conference's larger churches near the campus? What were her plans concerning family in the future? Did she have a significant other? Didn't she find college life greatly different from her experience in a small rural high school? Had she done any public speaking in college? Had she ever spoken before a large group, other than to her peers in the conference youth fellowship?

The questioning went on for some time without really engaging the written material Jane had submitted, which included statements of her personal faith, her sense of call, and her commitment to the denomination's doctrine and government. In fact, the chairperson called for a close to the interview before any of that was ever lifted up for discussion. Jane was asked to leave the room and wait outside while the committee consulted on her application.

After Jane left the room, none of the committee members spoke; the room was silent except for the shuffling of papers and one person clearing his throat. Finally, the chairperson spoke. The application was before them; they had spoken with the candidate. What thoughts did anyone wish to share before a vote was taken?

"Do we have any currently active clergy who have come from the same congregation as this candidate?" asked one of the members.

"I don't think so," answered another. "It's been a solid witness in its community for many years, but that church has never done anything remarkable."

Another member, who had been on the committee when Jane's exploring candidacy had been approved three years before, spoke up. "I don't know. She's a good worker and obviously a committed Christian. She would make a wonderful pastor's spouse."

"That's rather sexist, don't you think?" snapped one of the two female committee members.

"I didn't say 'wife'," the offender quickly responded. "I just don't think this young woman, coming from her background, is going to have the savvy to stand up to the rigors of the pastorate — especially in a larger church."

The other woman on the committee quickly followed up, asking, "Is it because she's a woman, or because she's a country-bumpkin?"

Hearing that the proceeding was headed in a bad direction, the chairperson broke in. "Who offered letters of recommendation for Jane's certification? Everyone has a copy of her material. Is there anything that stands out about her gifts for ministry from those who spoke for her?"

After some further shuffling of papers, a committee member, who hadn't previously spoken, referenced Jane's recommendation from the conference's youth advisor, a pastor at one of the leading churches. "Frank Borland states in his letter that Jane is a great organizer and is popular with her peers."

"That seems hardly adequate," responded the member who thought Jane would make a good clergy spouse.

"Well, the other letters from Jane's pastor and from the council president of her congregation state that Jane has a love for the Lord and what they see as definite gifts of the Holy Spirit for ministry," stated the committee's recording secretary. From there, the conversation continued among the committee members. While the discussion moved away from direct reference to Jane's background and gender, which pleased the chairperson, those issues continued to be the backdrop for a conversation concerning Jane's candidacy that did not lead to consensus within the group. Finally, the chairperson called for an end to the discussion.

"We can vote to approve, to deny, or to defer the application for future consideration," the chairperson informed the committee. "We will vote by written ballot." When the ballots were all passed to the recording secretary and counted, the results were reported.

"One to deny, three to approve, five for deferral," announced the secretary.

Jane felt numb during the remaining drive home after the committee shared with her its decision on deferring her certification. She wondered what more she would have had to do or say in order for her candidacy to be certified. What Jane didn't do was question the authenticity of her call. She knew her gifts and graces and been affirmed by people among whom her ministry sharing the love of God and the gospel of Jesus Christ had been done. She knew who she was and she knew what she was about. She knew God was working through her, and those who had encountered her ministry and had been transformed through it knew that, too.

When she arrived home her parents wanted to console her, but Jane did not want to feel sympathy. "They will have to make up their minds," she said to her folks about the Committee on Ministry. "I will be back in front of them," she said, "I'm not going away."

Sunday at church, between the Sunday school and worship hours, Jane had to tell the story of her experience with the committee several times. Some of the older folks expressed disbelief that her candidacy wasn't certified, and made remarks about their inability to understand church politics. Her friends with whom she grew up in church listened attentively to her story and encourage her not to give up.

"You and I know God's call is on you," Jane's friend, Rachel, was saying to her just as the pastor and lay leader came up to them. While Jane was not looking for sympathy from her pastor, she was hoping for something different than she got from him.

After telling him the story of her deferral in Rachel's presence, the pastor gave what Jane felt was a rather stock response. "I know this is deflating, Jane," he said, "but there is wisdom in our structures. You have to trust the process." When the pastor left them to head in to the sanctuary, Jane turned and looked at Rachel.

"I guess if the Bible isn't inerrant, the Conference Committee on Ministry must be. Order and structure is a good thing, but it often seems to be an obstacle to the Holy Spirit instead of the Spirit's instrument."

Rachel smiled. "At least you're in good company, Jane," she said. "This must have been how Jesus felt when he encountered the unbelief of those in authority."

John 9:1-41

Our Need To Belong

We all have a need to belong. How we find that need satisfied makes all the difference in how we live our lives. The need to belong is particularly acute in young people, who are just finding their place in the world. However, all of us at whatever age have a deep emotional need to feel included, having a place and a group to belong.

Sometimes belonging can be experienced in multiple circles. We can at one and the same time belong to a bridge club, a fire company, and the Loyal Order of Moose without a conflict. None of these groups demand our undivided allegiance, but neither do they give to our lives ultimate meaning. Belonging that gives our lives significance and ultimate meaning is a singular belonging, a choice between competing allegiances and lifestyles that are mutually exclusive.

In the gospel according to John, we are confronted with the choice to belong to the old order, the old world, or to belong to Jesus and the new world that is being brought into being in him. The Evangelist confronts us with this choice of belonging through the people who encounter Jesus. As we read the stories of these encounters, we find ourselves personally relating to the characters in a way that makes their struggles and choices our own. The story of the man born blind works this way.

Not unlike the paralytic at the pool of Bethzatha, the man born blind finds that his healing by Jesus brings crisis and complication into his life. He is hauled before the Pharisees because Jesus healed him on the sabbath. A debate subsequently erupts concerning the source of Jesus' healing power. Can he be from God if he heals on the Sabbath?

As exhibit "A", the formerly blind man is required to state his position on Jesus. Unsatisfied with the man's testimony that Jesus is a prophet, the Pharisees even disbelieve that the man was blind from birth and they summon his parents.

"Is this your son?" they asked. "Do you say that he was blind from birth? How is it that he can see now?" (John 9:19).

The man's parents acknowledged that he was indeed their son and that he was born blind. "But we do not know how it is that now he sees, nor do we know who opened his eyes," they told their interrogators. "Ask him; he is of age. He will speak for himself" (John 9:20-21).

Why were they so evasive? "They were afraid of the Jews," states the Evangelist, "for the Jews had already agreed that anyone who confessed Jesus to be the Messiah would be put out of the synagogue" (John 9:22-23).

The couple left their son on his own. It was not something they wanted to do, really. They felt forced to make an unattractive choice. But their need to continue to belong to the synagogue was strong. Their whole identity was probably wrapped up in the synagogue and their self-understanding as observant Jews. Their son's sight was a wonderful gift — probably a gift that could only come through one who was closer to God than any other person. But the choice between acknowledging him as the Messiah could come only at the cost of being ejected from the synagogue community. It was a price they were unwilling to pay.

The formerly blind man was then summoned again by the Pharisees, who implicitly required him to denounce Jesus. "Give glory to God!" they demanded, "We know this man is a sinner" (John 9:24). But the man who had been blind now saw in more ways than one. He saw the truth to which both the Pharisees and his parents remained obstinately blind. His unwillingness to submit to the demands of the Pharisees caused him to be put out of the synagogue, but his awakened spiritual sight led him to confess Jesus as Messiah. Seeing eyes opened a world to him, but a perceiving spirit opened to him a new world. He would not surrender his place in this new world in order to satisfy the old ways of the elders.

With which character or characters in this story do you relate? Before you decide, let me share a personal story of something I experienced and did many years ago.

I was employed as an electrician trainee in a steel mill. One winter, business slowed dramatically and maintenance was required to trim staff. Being the least senior member of the electrical department, I was furloughed. However, I had enough plant seniority to "bump" into one of the production shops as a laborer. I was sent to a machine shop for second-shift cleanup duty.

I had been working in the machine shop about two weeks when one night, while on break, one of the lathe operators asked me, "Are you a Christian?" His question took me completely by surprise, and I was not sure where his question might be leading. He certainly did not seem to be asking as one Christian to another. I didn't understand where he was coming from.

"No, I'm not a Christian. Why would you think I'm a Christian?" I asked him.

"Well, that electrician gang is a rough lot," he replied, "and you don't seem to act like most of them. I thought maybe it was because you are a Christian."

I felt my insides drop. I was a Christian then, but I was also working among an unfamiliar group of men in a new environment. I desperately wanted to fit in, to belong, and I was afraid that my profession of Christ would mean they would exclude me. I deluded myself into thinking that I could not be seen as the outsider that I really was.

I left work that night at eleven o'clock, ashamed and feeling more outcast than ever. Denying Christ had not gained for me any respect from my new co-workers, and I had grieved the Holy Spirit. Across the thirty years since then I have never forgotten the lathe operator's question that night, or my reply. But although our love may fail, I can only give thanks that God's love and forgiveness remain steadfast for us. Other opportunities to profess Christ as Lord have come along, and making a different reply has made all the difference.

Where do you see yourself in the story of the man born blind? With which character or characters do you relate? Are you the spiritually newly sighted, who would not trade for anything your glimpse of the new world and your new life in Christ? Do you feel like one of the Pharisees, desperately clinging to your advantages in the old order of things against all opposition — even opposition from the truth? Are you like the parents, whose profession may cost you the price of belonging among old friends and family situations? We all have a need to belong, but how we find that need satisfied makes all the difference in our lives — all the difference in the world.

John 10:1-15

We Are A Shepherded People

A metaphor is a figure of speech containing an implied comparison, in which a word of phrase...ordinarily used of one thing is applied to another. But a mixed metaphor is one that leaps from a first identification to a second identification inconsistent with the first. Take these, for example:

"You've buttered your bread, now lie in it."
"We'll burn that bridge when we come to it."
"A rolling stone is worth two in the bush."
"A stitch in time is worth a pound of cure."

Mixed metaphors can tickle our funny bones. But sometimes mixed metaphors aren't as mixed up as they may seem. Jesus employs what seems to be mixed metaphor in John 10. He speaks of himself as simultaneously being shepherd and the gate to the sheepfold. But in exploring this text further, we find that the two metaphors are in some ways synonymous, and they reassure us that we are a shepherded people.

We ought to begin by seeking to understand a little about what Palestinian shepherds did in Jesus' day, and still do, and how they work.

A shepherd's job required some simple, but staple, equipment. It included a shoulder bag of animal skin in which the shepherd carried his food and personal belongings. The food in a shepherd's scrip would be simple fare, perhaps no more than bread and cheese. He carried a *sling*, such as we read of the Benjaminites of the Old Testament using in battle, or of David using to fell the Philistine giant, Goliath. Shepherds needed to be practiced and accurate with the sling in order to defend themselves and their flock from thieves and wild animals. Also used in defense of person and flock was the *staff*: a short, wooden club used in close combat. It hung from the shepherd's belt by a leather thong passed through a slot in the handle. He also carried a *rod*, sometimes called the shepherd's *crook*. He might use it to hook a straying sheep and lead it back into the right path.

For safety at night, the shepherd would lead his sheep into a *sheepfold*: a pen constructed out of readily available and primitive materials. In the morning, the shepherd would lead out his sheep from the sheepfold to the day's pasturing. He would call to them and encourage them to follow where he led. The sheep would follow no one but their own shepherd, whose voice they recognized. If a stranger tried to lead the sheep or call to them, they would run away in alarm.

The Pharisees, to whom Jesus was speaking the words we find in this passage from the Gospel, should have been familiar with all of this, but they failed to get it. Perhaps they didn't want to get it, because in reality Jesus was continuing a rebuke of their leadership that he had begun earlier. The Pharisees claimed to be shepherds of God's flock. But in John 9, we read of the man born blind whom Jesus healed. Rather than care for this man pastorally, they tyrannically and mercilessly drove him from their synagogue. They were more concerned with maintaining their theological authority than with the spiritual and physical wellbeing of this sheep of Israel's fold.

In our world, we are perhaps more familiar with cattle than with sheep. You *drive* cattle. We ought to note the metaphor of leadership inherent in the Palestinian shepherd, who *leads* sheep by going ahead of them and calling them to follow. A lot of leadership in our world today — whether in business, civic organizations, or the church — seems to take its model from cattle ranching. In fact, we ought to change the title of many from "leader" to "driver." Think about how we talk of people "running" an organization or company—even a local church. This was Jesus' criticism of the leadership of the Pharisees. He said of them to his disciples,

"They tie up heavy burdens, hard to bear, and lay them on the shoulders of others; but they themselves are unwilling to lift a finger to move them" (Matthew 23:4). We are not a driven people; we are shepherded people. Jesus does not drive, but rather leads in the manner of the good shepherd. He goes ahead of us and proves the way. He calls us to follow. How different is his spiritual leadership from that which we experience in many aspects of our lives! He is the model for all authentic leadership that puts the wellbeing of others ahead of any personal gain of the leader.

Next, we need to notice that the voice of the shepherd is known to his sheep and it is discernible from the voice of strangers. It is well documented in the Middle East that sheep know and understand their shepherd's voice and respond solely to him. Sheep and shepherd may spend years together when the sheep are kept chiefly for wool. They build a relationship.

When I was a boy, my father hunted small game and kept a rabbit dog. It was a female beagle he had gotten as a puppy and named "Beauty." Dad whistled to call Beauty. It was a very lyrical tune that he had composed himself and whistled only when he wanted to call the dog. Beauty would leave a fresh rabbit trail — something completely counter to instinct — and run to my father when she heard his distinctive whistle. However, none of this came about quickly or naturally. Dad spent hours in cultivating a special relationship with Beauty. I could mimic Dad's whistle, but Beauty would not respond to me, because it wasn't with me that her relationship of dog-to-master had been cultivated.

We are not people remote from God. We are a shepherded people, because the one whom we call Lord seeks to be in relationship with us. Relationship is the key to his shepherding leadership. Being a Christian disciple is not a matter of following a particular set of practices, rules, or philosophy of life except and only as these are part and parcel of being in relationship with Jesus and others who heed the call to discipleship.

Again, we might compare the shepherding of Jesus to other kinds of leadership we experience in the world. Do others we acknowledge as leaders seek to be in meaningful relationship with us? Is that relationship inherent to their leadership, or is it just a happy happenstance when and if it occurs? Certainly there are acknowledged leaders with whom we would never reasonably expect to have a close relationship. But isn't it reassuring to know that the one to whom we look first for leadership of our souls is one who knows us deeply, who desires to be in relationship with us personally, and who calls us by name?

But about this mixed metaphor I mentioned earlier — Jesus identifies himself as the good shepherd, and he also claims the identity of gate to the sheepfold. Are these two metaphors antithetical? Let's think once more about the work of the Palestinian shepherd.

As mentioned, when sheep were being pastured out on the hillsides of Judean Palestine, they were brought at night into sheepfolds. "These hillside sheepfolds were just open spaces enclosed by a wall. In them, there was an opening by which the sheep came in and went out; but there was no door of any kind. What happened was that at night the shepherd himself lay down across the opening, and no sheep could get out or in except over his body."[2] So the shepherd and the door to the sheepfold are, in fact, synonymous.

Scottish theologian and Hebrew scholar, Sir George Adam Smith, has written of his encounter with a shepherd and his sheep in Palestine. The shepherd showed him the sheepfold consisting of four walls and a door-less entryway. When Smith noted that there was no door to keep the sheep in at night, the shepherd responded by saying, "I am the door. When the light has gone and all the sheep are inside, I lie in that open space. No sheep ever goes out but across my body, and no wolf ever comes in unless he crosses my body.

2   William Barclay, *The Gospel of John, Volume Two: The New Daily Study Bible* (Philadelphia: Westminster John Knox Press, 2001). 68.

I am the door."[3] Without perhaps knowing it, this shepherd had spoken the words of Jesus.

In saying that we can "come in and go out" through him, Jesus was using an old Hebrew phrase that described a way of life that was absolutely secure and safe. When people can "go in and out" without fear means that they are perfectly secure. Immediately after speaking of himself using this phrase, Jesus speaks of those who come to the sheepfold only as thieves to kill and destroy. In the context of his day he was speaking of messianic pretenders who promised a new golden age through bloodshed and violence. He was speaking of zealots and other political radicals, who sought to overthrow the Romans by force and establish a purified Jewish theocracy in Judea.

Militant theology and confrontational rhetoric are not peculiar to first century Palestine. We live in a world populated by movements and ideologues, which promise glory and power to whoever will become a follower. Militant religion and the rhetoric of violence are not only to be found in radical Islam. We see in our American political landscape the abuse of religion, strident political positioning, and the use of provocative language that divides us from each other as citizens, polarizes Christianity, and paralyzes effective government — all by people grasping for power and promising greater security and abundance to those who will support them.

We are not a martial people; we are shepherded people. We do follow one who did not open his mouth when oppressed, but went like a lamb to the slaughter. He is the Good Shepherd through whom we come in and go out in peace. Not through force or military might, not through bristling politics or strident positioning, but through his self-offering even unto death we receive abundant life. He is

3   Quoted in W. Robert Willoughby, *John: Believing in the Son* (Camp Hill, PA: Christian Publications, 1999). 194-195.

the gate to the sheepfold where we have security that transcends mortality, and an abundance of life that is greater than worldly wealth. We are a shepherded people.

We are not relentlessly driven on in life by impersonal forces. We are lovingly cared for by the God who knows us by name. We are not defended by one who uses violence and bloodshed, and who kills and destroys for the sake of his power. We are guarded by the Christ whose power is love, in which he enfolds us. He surrenders himself unto death and is to us the door to abundant life. We are his shepherded people.

John 10:22-39

Communication Success

"What we have here is a failure to communicate." That's one of the most quoted movie lines in history. It comes from one of my favorite films, *Cool Hand Luke*. *Cool Hand Luke* is a film with a great deal of theological content, but its theology can be pretty subtle.

Many of us would not look for Christian themes of resistance to oppression, of salvation, and of redemptive suffering in a film about prison life in the American South of the 1940s. But it's all there. However, you need to be open to looking for it through the imagery of the film. You have to allow your imagination some space to appropriate the movie's meaning for yourself, and that's something some folks won't allow themselves to do.

Perhaps the line from the movie I quoted is a paradoxical message about the movie itself. "What we have here is failure to communicate." The line is first spoken by the character of the prison warden, who is known simple as "Captain." After Luke Jackson, the movie's hero, attempts escape, he is recaptured, fitted in leg irons, and brutally punished as an example. As the other prisoners watch Luke suffer, the Captain delivers a warning speech to them beginning with the famous line, "What we have here is a failure to communicate. Some men you just can't reach."

Ironically, Luke parrots the Captain's line back to him near the end of the movie. Luke has escaped for the third time, and has been tracked down. He is trapped in a church, of all places. Just before he is shot to death by the chain gang foreman, Boss Godfrey, Luke cries out to the Captain, "What we have here is a failure to communicate."

It wasn't Luke who didn't understand. He knew what the Captain and the prison system he represented were all about and what they demanded. In parroting the line back to the Captain, Luke made it clear that it was the Captain who didn't understand. The prison system required inmates to surrender their souls. The message of the warden and the prison system had, indeed, reached Luke, but he rejected the message. He might have to surrender his life to the system, but he would not surrender his soul.

"What we have here is failure to communicate. Some men you just can't reach." Maybe the movie's message doesn't reach people because it comes to them in a way that is objectionable to their religious sensibilities. That seems to have been the problem with those religious leaders who accosted Jesus at the temple on the portico of Solomon during Hanukkah.

"How long will you keep us in suspense? If you are the Messiah, tell us plainly," they demanded. Be concrete. Be literal. Make a flat, straightforward declaration. That's what they wanted from Jesus. But he understood that their demand was not in order to believe. It was the demand for a statement that they could use against Jesus as a punishable blasphemy. He must fit their theological language; conform to their categories and fit into their descriptions. This is made clear by what immediately happens after Jesus said that he and the Father were one. The religious authorities prepared to stone him. "I have shown you many good works from the Father. For which of these are you going to stone me?" (v. 31). They answer that they did not find him guilty because of his works, but because he spoke so as to make himself equal with God.

The religious people had their ears tuned to hear blasphemy. They couldn't hear anything else Jesus said. Even though he used imagery from the sacred writings with which they were all familiar, speaking of himself in terms of the good shepherd depicted throughout scripture and most explicitly in Psalm 23, they couldn't be reached. They refused to allow their imaginations some space to appropriate for themselves the meaning of what Jesus was saying. "What we have here is failure to communicate."

Jesus' message didn't reach the authorities because it came to them in a way that was objectionable to their rigid hearts. In fact, his words might even seem objectionable to us. Jesus responded to their charge of blasphemy, saying "Is it not written in your law, 'I said you are gods?' If those to whom the word of God came were called 'gods' — and the scripture cannot be annulled — can you say that the one whom the Father has sanctified and sent into the world is blaspheming because I said, 'I am God's Son?' " (vv. 34-36).

Can these words be objectionable to us — to our flat, literal, understandings of orthodox belief? After all, "those to whom the word of God came" includes us, especially if we confess Jesus is the word of God. Therefore, according to Jesus, the scripture states that God declares to us, "I said you are gods." Is it objectionable to us to accept that designation, given that typically we maintain a pretty well defined dividing line between ourselves and divinity?

You can't help but be offended at what Jesus' implies in those words if you read them as a literal, concrete, straightforward description. But, if you will allow your imagination some space to appropriate for yourself the meaning of what Jesus was saying, you receive a gift. In classic Christian theological language, faith seeks understanding. What we receive in faith we appropriate as understanding when we do not close our minds to God's innovative and creative new avenues of revealing himself and drawing near to us.

The Bible uses shepherd imagery for God a lot. I don't have any experience with sheep or shepherding. In doing genealogical research, I learned that the occupation of my first ancestor on these shores was the work of a fuller. A fuller is someone who combs raw wool, cleans it, bleaches it, and pre-shrinks and thickens wool cloth. I had to look up what a fuller does. I had no idea. So I've had to work at this imagery of shepherd and sheep and reinterpret it for myself in order to understand and appropriate it for a fuller faith — no pun intended!

I have no personal experience of shepherds and sheep. But I do have experience as a steel mill electrician. On repair jobs electricians were sent out two-by-two, a less experienced electrician with a journeyman. When you were the less experienced person, you relied on your journeyman. He guided you in your work, taught you "tricks of the trade," shared his experience. A good journeyman also watched out for you, let you know where hidden dangers might be, and shielded you from the wrath of the department bosses if you made a mistake.

So I don't think about Jesus in terms of shepherd imagery, and when I read passages like this one from John I think of Jesus as my accompanying journeyman. I imagine Jesus going with me in the work of the day, barking at me at times when I'm not paying attention, teaching me the tricks-of-the-trade in discipleship, pointing out the dangers to my soul, and shielding me when I sinfully err.

Some folks, I'm sure, would have their rigid religious categories offended by how I own my relationship with Jesus. It doesn't completely square with some creedal statements perhaps. I'll admit that. All imagery and analogy falls short somewhere. Maybe it makes Jesus and me too equal, too much on par with each other. I remember arguing with my journeyman electrician on more than one occasion, and not feeling wrong about it. But, hey — it was Jesus who quoted the Scripture, "I said you are gods." If my reinterpretation of the sheep and shepherd relationship lends understanding to my faith and gives it a language that lets me better articulate my relationship with Jesus, I'm comfortable with that.

What ways do you need to let your imagination free in order to better own your relationship with Jesus? What creative imagery from your personal experience can you use to grasp God's message in Christ, to open your faith to a deeper understanding?

Maybe it's thinking of Jesus in the context of a nurturing grandmother. Maybe it's picturing Jesus in terms of a beloved scoutmaster from your past. Maybe Jesus is a wise elder brother. Among the medieval Christian mystics there is a revered tradition of imaging Jesus as the most intimate of lovers.

It is important to have creedal statements and official theological language. But we also need to have our own language, our own voice, and our own images by which to receive the message of God in Jesus Christ and to claim our relationship with him personally. Our thinking, our believing, our theologizing must be in terms faithful to our own experience of God and our world. Anything less is a failure to communicate.

John 11:1-44

Lazarus Raised

A great deal of attention and study is given to our high-stress contemporary culture and its effects upon human beings. Bath oils, herbal teas, and a myriad of self-help books are marketed as aids for coping with the high stress of the technologically driven, rapid-change society in which we live. Stress certainly is an issue for us. However, I think it can be helpful to distinguish stress from anxiety.

Anxiety and stress are related, but they are distinct from one another. Stress is an external circumstance; anxiety is an internal response. Stress can trigger anxiety, but a lot of anxiety is simply part and parcel of fallen human nature. The story of Jesus raising Lazarus from the dead deals with the three most problematic kinds of anxiety we experience. The first of these is the anxiety of delay, or waiting.

Twenty-first century Americans do not typically cope well with waiting — for anything. We are an instant-gratification society. We do not like public transportation, because it means standing in line with others waiting to board a bus or train rather than taking our personal automobile according to our own time schedule. I remember when we only had an electric range, and I was perfectly happy to wait for food to cook on the range top. Once we got a microwave oven, which would cook most food in a fraction of the time a conventional range requires, I began impatiently watching the oven timer count down the seconds until my food is hot. Personal computers have been obsoleted at a record pace as we have sought faster and faster log-on speeds. The more quickly things can be done, the more impatient we become.

Mary and Martha watching their brother sink slowly into death while waiting for Jesus to come to his aid is almost unbearable to think about. The anxiety these two women must have felt, knowing that Jesus had the power to heal Lazarus but seeing him die as Jesus delayed, is incomprehensible for us. Why did Jesus make them wait?

Very simply stated, Jesus delayed for the sake of the glory of God. Put another way, Jesus had in mind a greater work in the lives of Mary, Martha, Lazarus, and their neighbors than healing Lazarus while alive could achieve. He had healed before. Those involved with Lazarus' illness understood Jesus had the power to heal. What they did not yet fathom was that, in Jesus, the very power and essence of life resided. Believing in Jesus as a great healer and teacher is not the same as believing in Jesus as God the Son in whom dwells the very power of life over death. The second belief is greater, and it leads to salvation and the glorification of God in the life of the believer. It was this kind of belief that Jesus evoked in the lives of Mary, Martha, and some of their neighbors by waiting and allowing Lazarus to die and then restoring him to life.

Waiting in prayer is, I think, akin to the waiting of Mary and Martha. If you pray, you will experience the anxiety of waiting. We have those people or circumstances that keep us in loving concern, distress, and pain. We earnestly pray for God to act, to intervene, to initiate some change that will relieve our anxiety. But God delays. We may begin to think that God's delay is arbitrary, or that there is some test involved for us in the delay. I believe the more likely thing is that God is telling us to wait, for through the delay God will achieve a greater good than the good most obvious to us. The greater good God seeks will bring us to a deeper level of belief and a greater glorification of God in our lives.

The second great anxiety of contemporary life is the anxiety of uncertainty. What's going to happen next? I think this kind of anxiety became even more acute for Americans after September 11, 2001. Much of the official response from government to the events of that day and the circumstances surrounding them served to keep Americans in a continuing state of uncertainty. What is the current threat code? Is it yellow, orange, or red? What does any of that mean, really? What might happen to us?

When Jesus finally decided to make the trip to Judea after hearing of Lazarus' illness, the disciples' response demonstrated their anxiety of uncertainty. "Rabbi," they said to him, "the temple hierarchy was looking to stone you on your last visit there, and are you now returning?" What happens if you go back, Jesus? Do the authorities manage to carry out their designs for you this time? And what might happen to us?

Jesus assured them that the forces of darkness have no ultimate power over those who walk in the presence of the world's light. Only those who employ the power of darkness have reason to fear, because such people do not have the light inside them.

What gives you assurance amid your anxiety about the uncertainty of our world? Do you feel more secure behind the power of military might? Does force really deliver peace? Isn't it absurd to think that warfare will protect our world from violence? In Psalm 20 we read, "Some take pride in chariots, and some in horses, but our pride is in the name of the LORD our God. They will collapse and fall, but we shall rise and stand upright."

Those who make their journey through this world in the company of Jesus Christ go with a greater assurance of well being than any army can provide. Armed defense offers protection, but no guarantee, against being harmed. Walking with Christ will not guarantee that no physical harm will befall you, but Christ guarantees something greater: transcendent victory over whatever harm the forces of darkness can devise. Living in the company of Christ Jesus, we have power over the anxiety of uncertainty.

As distressing as these anxieties of waiting and uncertainty may be, they pale to the great anxiety of human existence: the anxiety of death. Humans alone among living beings have the ability to apprehend the knowledge of the inevitability of our own deaths. This is something that sets us apart from all other creatures.

I have a housecat named Sylvester. Although he lacks my powers of speech, he can communicate. Like me, Sylvester can show affection and other emotions. However, Sylvester can't know something I know: both he and I are going to die. Sylvester lives moment to moment. I live every moment in the shadow of my oncoming death.

The anxiety of death is really the parent of all our other anxieties. It casts a shadow over everything we do. The concerns of contemporary society — health care, national security, sexuality, abortion, terrorism, and the rest — all have their roots in the anxiety of death. In the face of the anxiety of death, God the Son says to us as he said to Martha, the sister of Lazarus, "I am the resurrection and the life. Those who believe in me, even though they die, will live, and everyone who lives and believes in me will never die. Do you believe this?" (John 11:25-26).

You can go on living in anxiety, waiting in fear, fearing uncertainty, or you can live and walk in the presence of the light. You can place your trust in the powers of the world, or you can place your trust in the one who is the resurrection and the life. The first way issues into an eternal, tomb-shrouded existence called death. But, for those who follow the second way, even though they die, they will live.

Do you believe this?

John 12:1-8

Timely Love

The Gift of the Magi may be the most enduring short story written by the master of the short story, William Sidney Porter, who is known popularly under the pen name of O. Henry. In *The Gift of the Magi*, a young couple, Della and Jim, are very poor but very much in love. Each has one unique possession. Della's hair is her glory. When she let it down, it almost served as a robe. Jim has a gold watch, which had come to him from his father, and is his pride.

It is the day before Christmas, and Della has exactly $1.87 to buy Jim a present. Knowing that such a paltry amount is insufficient to provide a gift that will appropriately express her love, she goes out and sells her hair for twenty dollars. With the proceeds, she buys a platinum fob for Jim's precious watch.

When Jim arrives home that night, and sees Della's shorn head, he is stupefied. It's not that he doesn't like it or that he no longer loves her; to him, she is lovelier than ever. Slowly he hands her his gift: a set of expensive tortoise-shell combs with jeweled edges for the long hair she no longer has. He has purchased the combs with the proceeds realized from the sale of his watch. Each gave to the other all there was to give. Real love cannot think of any other way of giving.

Such is the giving of Mary of Bethany in John 12. It is just six days before the Passover, on the eve of the day prescribed by the Law of Moses that sacrificial lambs were to be selected for the Passover feast. Jesus has come to the house of his friends, Mary, Martha, and Lazarus in Bethany. His time was nearing its end, his mission nearing completion. Within a week he would be crucified.

Jesus' friends at Bethany had given a dinner in his honor, but we might assume that it was not a particularly festive occasion. The chief priests had issued a warrant for Jesus' arrest should he appear in Jerusalem for Passover. Lazarus, whom Jesus had raised from the grave, was at the dinner with him. The evangelist bore witness that the chief priests were seeking to put Lazarus to death, as well, "because on account of him many of the Jews were going away and believing in Jesus" (John 12:10-11). The mood in the house was undoubtedly foreboding.

Perhaps it was the unbearable tension that led Mary to her provocative act. Taking a pound jar of perfumed ointment costing the equivalent of a year's wages for a laborer, she anointed Jesus' feet with it. Moreover, she cast aside all norms of decency in letting down her hair — an act forbidden for a Jewish woman in the presence of any man other than her husband — and used her unbound tresses to wipe Jesus' feet. It is an act of love that surrenders everything, including her public respectability.

At Mary's act of love, Judas Iscariot chafed and challenged its propriety. It's not her surrender of female decency to which he objected, but her extravagant use of the costly ointment. "Why was this perfume not sold for three hundred denarii and the money given to the poor?" (John 12:5). Never mind the evangelist's commentary that Judas was thinking only of being able to lift the proceeds for himself from the common purse. His comment reflecting an attitude of coldly calculated charity was enough.

The scene at the house in Bethany less than a week before the crucifixion calls us to reflect on our response to God's goodness in our lives. Do we return to God with Mary's kind of extravagant love, or is our response one of coldly calculated charity? What is the inner motivation for our giving? Is it the outpouring of a deeply grateful heart, or the measured response of a conscience seeking to assuage the guilt of having much more than 80% of the world's wealth?

While the Bible offers the tithe as the basis for our personal giving in response to God, we note that Jesus was less concerned about our measure of giving than our motivation for giving. He applauded the overflowing heart of a poor widow, whose superabundant love was represented by two copper coins, over the copious monetary gifts of the rich being dropped into the temple treasury (cf. Luke 21:1-4; Mark 12:41-44). Mary's extravagant gift of love in anointing Jesus was no doubt at least partly inspired by his miraculous gift of returning the life of her brother, Lazarus. Is our giving motivated by religious obligation or by the realization of the new life we have in Jesus?

Judas' challenge was not only an attack on Mary's act of love, but it was also an accusation of hypocrisy against Jesus. It was as if Judas was saying to him, "You, who proclaim a ministry of release to the captives and the bringing of good news to the poor, will you call us to lives of self-denial while indulging yourself? Isn't your willingness to spend this perfumed ointment like this really making it worse on the poor?"

We see this kind of thing happen all the time in our world. In 2008, former Vice President Al Gore was interviewed on a radio show about his stand on the dangers of global warming. Hard questions were raised, objections were answered, but the talk stayed on topic. The next day a caller phoned in with criticism. He did not challenge the science of global warming or the veracity of Gore's claims. The caller criticized Gore for flying a jetliner to Europe to receive the Nobel Prize. The caller's point was that if Gore really believed in global warming he should prove it by staying home and not riding on a jet that contributed to atmospheric pollution.

There is a term for this kind of criticism. When you can't make your point reasonably, you substitute a personal attack. It's called argumentum ad hominem. It's an argument against the person. Attack, attack, attack, and distract, distract, distract.

Jesus would not be distracted. Nor did he allow Mary's love to be ridiculed. "Leave her alone. She bought it so that she might keep it for the day of my burial," he retorted. "You always have the poor with you, but you do not always have me" (John 12:8). Jesus focused on the timeliness of Mary's act of love, and he reminded us that, indeed, "for everything there is a season and a time for every matter under heaven" (Ecclesiastes 3:1).

Jesus quoted Deuteronomy 15:11, which directs the people that they are to care for the poor in their midst. It is realistic in its assessment that there will always be poor people in need, and that we should stay alert always to providing for those needs. But Jesus also made it clear that Mary had only a limited time in which she could directly offer him her gesture of love. His time was short; his death and burial were at hand. Mary's action acknowledged this, and expressed a depth of gratitude that went beyond all measure and all refined sense of respectability.

In a community where I once lived, a man thought to be a poor laborer without any family and who always put out large gardens around his ramshackle home, died and left a surprising five million dollar estate to be divided among four area congregations. The sad thing was that all of these churches were poor and struggling, and one had in fact ceased to exist before the windfall inheritance could come to it. How much love might this man had known and engendered had he given his gift along the way instead of holding out until he was dead?

It has been said somewhere that our lack of time to express love and appreciation to those who mean the most to us will always be made up by more than enough time later to regret not having done so. Even the Son of God did not assume upon time, and he always grasped the eternal significance of the moment and how it was spent.

Let us love extravagantly without measure in response to God's immeasurable love. Let us live with an uncritical eye, seeing only the goodness of what others have to offer. Let us use the time now to give fully of ourselves to others, trusting in the immeasurable life we have with God through Jesus Christ.

John 12:12-19

Humble Entry

"His disciples did not understand these things at first; but when Jesus was glorified, then they remembered that these things had been written of him and had been done to him" (John 12:16).

What Jesus did didn't make sense to them. He was always doing this sort of thing. Just when the situation looked like it was time to throw the fastball, Jesus delivered the curve and cast everything in a different perspective.

It took no time at all for the news about the raising of Lazarus to be broadcast throughout Jerusalem. Everyone heard that this man from Galilee, about whom it was already rumored that he might be the Messiah, had called forth a dead man from his tomb out in Bethany. It was the greatest of the signs he had performed, and for many people it no longer left any question about his being the Messiah. But what kind of Messiah was he?

Many people were living in anticipation of the Messiah, but with certain expectations about what the Messiah would be and what he would do. Many expected that he would rule as king over a revived Jewish state. He would put the subjugating Romans to flight. He would bring back the glories of Solomon's empire. He would make the Law of Moses the law of the land. He would cleanse the temple and restore the legitimate priesthood of Aaron.

"His disciples did not understand these things at first; but when Jesus was glorified, then they remembered that these things had been written of him and had been done to him" (John 12:16).

Oh, the disciples understood the parade all right. Everybody loves a parade! Nor was there any question about the palm branches on the road. Palm branches were a sign of Jewish nationalism. Waving palm branches before a parade welcoming Jesus into Jerusalem is like standing in Town Square, USA on the fourth of July and waving little American flags before the open convertible carrying some local war hero. But Jesus didn't ride in a convertible; he rode the foal of a donkey. It would have exemplified more imperial dignity if he had just walked.

"His disciples did not understand these things at first; but when Jesus was glorified, then they remembered that these things had been written of him and had been done to him" (John 12:16).

When it happened, it must have brought back bad memories of that day he had fed the multitude on the Golan Heights. Just when the crowd was ready to make him king, Jesus disappeared and left his disciples with a confused rabble of locals (cf. John 6:1-15). He had done it again! But they weren't off in the isolated regions of Galilee. They were at the gates of the Holy City. As the crowd waved their palms and cried out, "Hosanna!" and "Blessed is the one who comes in the name of the Lord, the king of Israel!" Jesus climbed on, of all things, a lowly donkey. It wasn't even full grown.

"The so-called triumphal entry was hardly a triumph. It was a shabby show in the carnival atmosphere of a religious festival: a simply dressed provincial rabbi and miracle worker on a borrowed donkey being welcomed noisily by an enthusiastic but frothy crowd."[4]

"His disciples did not understand these things at first; but when Jesus was glorified, then they remembered that these things had been written of him and had been done to him" (John 12:16).

Only then did they see the events of that Sunday as the fulfillment of a prophecy about the Messiah and understand that the royalty of Messiah Jesus differed radically

4   Lamar Williamson, Jr., *Preaching the Gospel of John: Proclaiming the Living Word* (Louisville: Westminster/John Knox Press, 2004). 148.

from what the world called glory. Jesus' glory was not revealed on a warhorse, or a golden throne. It was revealed on a cross and by an empty grave. Only through memory illumined by the event of Jesus' death and resurrection could the Palm Sunday ride on the donkey be understood, and the real glory that Jesus embodied — and to which he called his disciples — be grasped.

Have we grasped this kind of glory, the glory that Jesus calls his disciples to manifest in the world? When I hear how congregations compete with one another for denominational status or community prestige, I wonder. When I read about the outcry raised by Christians when scripture monuments are removed from courthouses and public parks but hear nary a whimper over the bloodshed caused by war, I wonder. When we build magnificent additions to our churches and call them family life centers but ignore the needs of the homeless or those in substandard housing, I wonder. When television evangelists strut across the stage in expensive clothes and glittering jewelry while missionaries are recalled from the field and furloughed because of a lack of funding, I seriously wonder.

"His disciples did not understand these things at first; but when Jesus was glorified, then they remembered that these things had been written of him and had been done to him" (John 12:16).

Today we will come to the table of our Lord. We will call the cup his shed blood and the bread his broken body. We will eat and drink at the command of Jesus, "Do this in remembrance of me." But will this act be part of an authentic remembering of the lowly Jesus, whose glory was seen in lowly, self-giving service or will our memory fail us? Will this week be a shabby show with the carnival atmosphere of religious festival, a parade at the one end and new spring clothes at the other, or will it truly be a Holy Week? Shall we embrace the glitter of the world, or the glory of Jesus?

John 13:31-38

Departure

Good night, good night! Parting is such sweet sorrow,
That I shall say good night till it be morrow.

Romeo and Juliet Act 2, scene 2
William Shakespeare

Juliet bid Romeo good night from her balcony. It was a prophetic good night that anticipated their tragic farewell in death. Such is the emotion of saying good bye or good night, a "sweet sorrow" that acknowledges the gratitude for love and the sorrow of separation. But something more, I think, inhabits every good-bye, for every good bye is anticipatory.

I have often told the story of an older co-worker from many years ago, who shared with me on a Monday morning that his weekend had been very busy. His son and daughter-in-law and their children had come for a visit.

"What's the best thing about your grandchildren visiting?" I asked. Without pause my co-worker replied, "Watching them wave good-bye out the back window of the car."

We both laughed. The part of the story I never tell is what happened next. That older co-worker, only a few months from retirement, got a far-away look in his eyes. Then, without looking at me, he said "Well, I'm only kidding. The day will come when I will no more see small hands wave good bye through that back window." He recognized the anticipatory nature of his grandchildren's farewells.

Jesus anticipated his departure with his disciples in the upper room. In the gospel according to John, he took a long time to say good bye. Nearly three whole chapters in the gospel are called Jesus' farewell discourse, beginning with our reading of John 13:31-38. Jesus did his very best to prepare his disciples for life in his physical absence. He gave them guidance about living together in community. He promised that they would be together again, that he would come and take them with him to where he was going. He promised that, until then, they would not be alone, but the Father would send the Holy Spirit to them as comforter and advocate. He told them that, in fact, they would do well if he did depart, so that the Spirit would come and lead them into even greater works. Jesus reassured them that they were ready for this physical separation from him.

Jesus anticipated his departure with his disciples, but their response indicated that the old cliché was true. We may anticipate the departure, the death, of someone we love, but we are never ready for it. Their death and disappearance from our physical world is really outside our ken to understand. We can very well say we know that all people die, but we can't fully grasp the import of that. Our head nods in knowing, but our heart shakes back and forth in denial.

Look at the disciples. Peter wanted to know exactly where Jesus intended to go. He seemed to understand that Jesus was talking about dying, and he made a rash promise that he would die too, he would lay down his own life for Jesus. But Jesus knew this bold promise was a response to the feelings of helplessness Peter was experiencing. Jesus confronted Peter's baseless promise for what it was, because it is not in keeping with what Jesus needed Peter to do and to be later. In the following chapters of this farewell discourse, Philip and Judas would both reveal their anxiety about what was happening (John 14:8, 22), and the disciples as a group will exhibit great distress and confusion about what Jesus was saying to them (John 16:17-18).

All good-byes are anticipatory of that separation we know in death. Parting is sweet sorrow only after some time passes. We can't even begin to miss someone we love but see no more until our pain settles, our emotions become less raw, and our sense of being violated eases. The word "bereaved" literally means "having been robbed." That's what death first hits us with. It's not a sweet sorrow, but a feeling of being violently abused — of having a vital part of our being ripped away. We are truly bereaved — robbed — of a relationship that gives us a sense of identity, of having a place in the world, of knowing who we are and what we are about.

The disciples' bewilderment and anxiety, their off-the-mark questions, rash promises, and demands for reassuring revelation were not strange, stupid, or proof that they just didn't get what Jesus is about. They were signs of their bereavement. Their responses were normal reactions to the grief they were already experiencing in anticipation, and would later experience fully during and after Jesus' crucifixion.

Parting can become a sweet sorrow, at best. But even that takes a great deal of time and healing. Parting at first is raw bereavement, "having been robbed," and it leaves us bewildered, anxious, and angry. It leads us to say and do things that seem irrational and make others, as well as ourselves, uncomfortable. It overwhelms us with feelings of helplessness and violation. Perhaps the most bizarre thing is that we call it normal. Yet it is normal, because it is an aspect of human relationship that we all encounter, albeit in our own personal and individual ways. And, yes, we will all come to that day when we will take our leave of others.

The entire last part of John, from John 13:31 through to the very end of the gospel might well be seen as Jesus grief counseling with his disciples. He anticipated his departure with them, reassured them of his love, and spoke words of comfort and peace to them. He gave them a ritual that transformed his relationship with them from a physical communion to a spiritual communion. He died on a cross, not in resignation but with acceptance. As the risen Lord, he came to them and guided them from dissolute inaction to purposeful living, and he granted them power for meaningful mission through the gift of the Holy Spirit.

We might see this section of John's gospel as a pattern for us when we are overtaken by grief and bereavement. God gives us words of reassurance, hope, and comfort in the scriptures. We can begin to develop our own rituals for transforming our relationship with the person who has died from a physical to a spiritual communion. We can begin to find that life is still meaningful, and we can realize the resources available to reengage life's activities with purpose. However, there is one thing above all that we need to hold on to through all of this.

When I was a young boy in the early grades of elementary school, my best friend was Charlie. Charlie and I were different in many ways, but he and I shared a bond that somehow went beyond mutual interests and similar family situations. Charlie was the youngest of three boys and I had two younger sisters. I liked sports, but Charlie wasn't very athletic because he had suffered rheumatic fever when he was a toddler. Charlie and I both were artistic in our own ways, and both of us enjoyed history. Perhaps that's what brought us to become such good friends.

Between fourth and fifth grade, my father put our home up for sale and made plans to move twenty miles away in order to be closer to where he worked. We prepared to move. I registered for school in the new town where we were going. Charlie and I spent whatever time together we could that summer, camping out in each other's back yards, fishing in a nearby creek, and drawing caricatures of each other and laughing.

The time came when our house sold and we packed to move. Charlie and I spent an afternoon together saying good-bye. We still laughed, but when it came time for me to go, it was hard. Charlie slipped a note in my hand and told me not to read it until I got to our new house. I promised that's what I would do, and we parted. It was not sweet sorrow.

When I arrived at our new house, everything seemed out of place. I couldn't find my things, and the house was full of boxes and confusion. As it got dark, I thought I was the most forlorn kid on the planet. I felt like crying, but I didn't want to. I took out the note Charlie had given me. It read: "When you're lonely, think about the night we put up the tent with the opening facing up hill and it rained. Keep smiling and make new friends. Remember I'm always your friend who truly loves you and will miss you. Write to me as soon as you can. Your friend, Charlie."

Charlie and I continued to write letters to each other throughout the fifth grade. I was able to make some new friends knowing that Charlie loved me as a friend and was always just a letter away. And the time came when Charlie and I were able to reunite. Our friendship was different then, but maybe stronger in a lot of ways.

Jesus gave his disciples a new commandment as he said good-bye: "Love one another." I think it was both a mission to accomplish and a strategy for living with hope and purpose beyond his physical presence. The love of God and love for one another is the constant to be maintained through all the craziness that is bereavement. It's what puts the sweet into even the sorrow of separation.

John 14:15-21

We Have Someone Called In

Ask the question, "What is love?" and you may get as many answers as there are people in the room. To a child, the test of love is her mother's hugs and kisses. To an adolescent or young adult it may be the infatuated attention of the lover. For someone of more maturity the test of love may be described as the going through thick and thin together. To the dog lover, the test of love may simply be the wagging tail.

To John the Evangelist the only test of love for God is obedience. It was by his obedience that Jesus showed his love for God, and it is by our obedience that we are called to show our love for Jesus. New Testament scholar, C. K. Barrett, has written: "John never allowed love to devolve into a sentiment or emotion. Its expression is always moral and is revealed in obedience."[5]

Many of us know all too well how there are those who declare their love with words, but who, at the same time, bring pain and heartbreak to those they claim to love. Children say they love their parents, but cause them endless grief and anxiety by their at-risk behaviors and carelessness with life. Husbands swear love for their wives, and wives say how much they love their husbands. Yet, by inconsiderate self-centeredness, irritability, and thoughtless unkindness they bring pain to one another. According to John the Evangelist, love for Jesus — like the love of Jesus — is not an easy thing. It is known only in true commitment demonstrated through obedience. However, Jesus does not leave us to struggle alone in the life of discipleship. He has sent us the Advocate.

5 Quoted in William Barclay, *The Gospel of John, Volume Two: The New Daily Study Bible* (Philadelphia: Westminster John Knox Press, 2001) 193.

Our *New Revised Standard Version Bible* uses the word Advocate to translate the Greek word *parakletos*, but *parakletos* is really untranslatable by a single English word. The King James renders it as Comforter, which is probably not a good translation for us today given how the meaning of the word comforter has changed through the centuries. The *Revised Standard Version* along with the *New International Version* uses the word Counselor. It is only as we examine closely the word *parakletos* in detail that we can grasp the true richness of the church's historic teaching on the Holy Spirit.

Parakletos literally translated means someone called in, but it is the context, the reason why the person is called in, which gives the word its distinctive flavor. The Greeks used the word in a wide variety of ways. A *parakletos* might be a person called in to give witness in a law court in someone's defense, or an advocate called in to plead the cause of someone under a charge that would issue in a serious penalty. A *parakletos* might be an expert called in to render advice in some difficult situation, or a person called in as a motivational speaker to the lift the courage of a band of dispirited soldiers. Today we think of those difficult medical cases that defy the diagnosis and treatment of fine doctors, so that a specialist who excels in such cases is called in to offer a greater level of expertise. Always a *parakletos* is someone called in to help in time of need or trouble.

Comforter was once a good translation of the word *parakletos*. It goes back to the fourteenth-century English Bible scholar John Wycliffe, who used it in his English translation of the scriptures. But in Wycliffe's day, the word had a wider range of meanings. It comes from the Latin word *fortis*, which means brave, and a comforter was someone who enabled some dispirited person, or persons, to be brave. Comfort today has to do almost entirely with alleviating pain or distress. A comforter is someone who sympathizes with us when we are hurting or sorrowful, or both. Certainly the Holy Spirit does that, but to limit the Spirit's ministry to comfort alone impoverishes our faith and understanding. Sometimes we talk of being able to cope with situations, and that is exactly the work of the Holy Spirit. The Spirit bolsters us where we are inadequate and empowers us to cope courageously with challenges. The Holy Spirit makes possible victorious living where on our own we would only know defeat. So, I believe that Jesus is telling us he is giving us a difficult task, a hard calling. He's sending us out on a challenging engagement, but he is going to call someone in, the *parakletos*, who guides us in what we are to do and gives us the power to do it.

Jesus went on to say that the world cannot recognize the Spirit. When Jesus speaks of the world here he means human beings in human society acting as if there is no God. The point of Jesus' saying is that we can only see what we are looking for. An astronomer will see far more in the sky than an untrained person. A botanist will see far more in a hedgerow than someone who doesn't know botany. Someone who knows art will see far more in a portrait than someone who remains ignorant of art. Someone who understands something about music will get far more out of a symphony than the person who has no real interest in music. Always what we see and experience depends on what we bring to the seeing and experiencing. A person who has eliminated God from the equation of life never listens for God. We cannot receive the Holy Spirit unless we wait in expectation and in prayer for the Spirit.

The Holy Spirit is no gatecrasher. The Spirit will enter when we are receptive. The Holy Spirit is *parakletos*: one called in, not one who forces in. When we think of the wonderful ministry of the Holy Spirit for us, will we not want to open our eyes and ears, our heart and soul, in expectant receptivity to the Spirit's entry?

John 14:23-29

Handsome Parting Gifts

Do you remember the old television game shows in which contestants competed for high luxury, big-money prizes — you know, like a refrigerator or $200 cash? Those were the days! My favorite memory of those shows is the rewards received by contestants who didn't win. A person might get an exotic assortment of jarred nuts or a year's supply of laundry detergent. The shows' producers had the audacity to call these thanks-for-playing send-offs handsome parting gifts.

That phrase, handsome parting gifts, has become a well-used metaphor in our culture. Last January, when retiring state congressmen were leaving office, our erstwhile, almost-daily newspaper (the only newspaper in our state capital and the only state capital city newspaper to print but three days per week) printed several articles about the fat pensions retiring state representatives and senators receive. Over and over again, the articles ridiculed the handsome parting gifts expected by folks who already had copious retirement resources.

Lifetime supplies of powdered bleach and featherbedding aside, no handsome parting gifts ever competed with those bestowed by Jesus upon the nascent church of first disciples in the upper room. They were certainly feeling like losers as Jesus continued to talk about his going away. He was the one departing, but they were receiving the gifts. Perhaps in that moment they could not appreciate the value of what he was giving them. But certainly these were gifts that keep on giving, for we, too, are the recipients of these gifts of grace that bestow upon us a spiritual identity, power for living, and a place within God's own heart.

In our gospel reading, Jesus says, "Those who love me will keep my word, and my Father will love them, and we will come to them and make our home with them" (John 14:23). At first blush, this may sound like tit-for-tat theology. It may sound like the Father's love for us is conditional, that it depends upon our ability to obey Jesus' word. Certainly holding fast to the word of the Lord is foundational for the Christian, but God's love for us is not dependent upon it. What Jesus is promising as his gift to his disciples is a reciprocal and reciprocating love between us and God the Father that includes Jesus as God's Son.

In Romans Paul writes, "God's love has been poured into our hearts through the Holy Spirit that has been given to us" (Romans 5:5). In other words, this love for God and keeping of Jesus' word begins with God. It begins with the Holy Spirit's ministry to us. It is through the Spirit that love for God is poured to overflowing into our hearts. This love for God within us opens wider the door of our hearts to receive even further God's love for us.

Another aspect of this reciprocating love is its unconditional nature. Elsewhere in Romans we read, "Indeed, rarely will anyone die for a righteous person — though perhaps for a good person someone might actually dare to die. But God proves his love for us in that while we still were sinners Christ died for us" (Romans 5:7-8).

There's a story that illustrates this kind of love on a human level. A family in north Georgia lived as sharecroppers. It was during the Great Depression. They had few of the niceties of life, but one year, after settling up with the farm owner, they had a small amount of money left over. It wasn't enough to buy something for each member of the family, so they had to decide on something the entire family could share. They decided to buy a mirror. Ten days after ordering it, their treasure arrived. They quickly tore open the box. The father was the first to look, and he frowned. The mother smiled when she looked, and the baby giggled.

The mirror was passed to Willie last. He looked, and didn't know whether to frown or cry.

When Willie was very small, he had been kicked in the face by a mule. His face had been left with an ugly, deforming scar. After seeing himself in the mirror, Willie turned to his mother and said, "Momma, did you know all along that I looked like this?"

"Yes, Willie," she answered, "of course I did."

"And you still loved me?" Willie asked, with tears now forming in his eyes.

"Yes, Willie, I still love you," She said. "The face don't make no difference. I love you because I know the boy behind the face."

That's the unconditional love that God has for us. God sees beyond the scars and through the ugliness of our sin and loves us with an unconditional, limitless, redeeming love. That's the same love we are given with which to love and care for others. It is, indeed, a handsome parting gift from Jesus to his disciples in every age. It is the gift that keeps on giving.

I'm going to risk the television allusions a little further by quoting from some of those commercials advertising products not offered in any store. Before you decide not to buy the product for only $9.99, the announcer says: "But wait! There's more!" Truly, with the parting gifts of Jesus there is more!

Jesus tells the disciples, "The Advocate...whom the Father will send in my name will teach you everything, and remind you of all that I have said to you" (John 14:26).

We probably wish we could take this word literally, that the Advocate — the Holy Spirit — would teach us *everything*. We could cure cancer, the common cold, and put an end to birth defects. Again, we need to apprehend what Jesus is saying with spiritual ears. He says, "The Advocate...will teach you everything, and remind you of all that I have said to you." Those two clauses, "everything...and all that I have said to you," are interconnected. The "everything" of which Jesus speaks is everything we need to know to be faithful disciples of Jesus.

At several places in the gospel of John the evangelist notes that, after Jesus was raised, the disciples remembered what Jesus had said and done and they could put what he taught into perspective for their ongoing growth in faith and understanding. The Holy Spirit gives the power to interpret the life and teaching of Jesus for application to our contemporary challenges and questions. We learn more about scripture through historical research and archaeology. We learn more about our world through science and technological advancement. Yet it is through the interpretive power of the Holy Spirit that we can appropriate and contextualize Jesus' teaching for our time and place.

And there is still more! Jesus gifts the disciples with, perhaps, the most precious of his handsome parting gifts. He says, "Peace I leave with you; my peace I give to you. I do not give to you as the world gives. Do not let your hearts be troubled, and do not let them be afraid" (John 14:27).

Is this the peace of continued good health? Hardly; we all still get sick, get injured, and die. Is this the peace of freedom from trouble? Not likely; we face hardships of all kinds: the loss of loved ones, broken marriages, troubled and troubling children, financial crises, and unhappiness of one kind or another. This is not peace that is escape from trials, but it is the peace of knowing that whatever trials we encounter we do not encounter them without God. Whatever we face, God is with us. Whatever befalls us cannot wrest us out of God's loving embrace. That kind of peace can only be known through the abiding presence of God's Holy Spirit.

In the days of the ancient Church, Eastern Christian monks lived ascetic lives together in community in the deserts of North Africa, Syria, and Palestine. In one of the desert monasteries all the brothers were impressed by the serenity and peace of the abbot. So taken were they with his behavior that at length they determined to question him about the source of his repose.

"We are harassed constantly by temptations," they told the abbot; "temptations that appeal to us so often and so strongly that they give us no rest. You seem to live untroubled by these things. Don't the temptations that harass our souls come knocking at the door of your heart?" they asked him.

The abbot replied: "My children, I do know of the things of which you speak. The temptations that trouble you do come, making their appeal to me. But, when they knock at the door of my heart, I answer, 'The place is occupied.' " The heart of the Christian disciple is at peace because the Holy Spirit dwells within.

Along with that troubled little group of disciples in the upper room, we are the recipients of the gifts of Jesus. We have the love of God poured out upon us and through us. It is a love that floods us with assurance, grants us the power to love God in return, and love our neighbor with God's unconditional love. It is love that opens us to the further gifts of the Spirit: the wisdom of discernment and that peace which passes all understanding. No disappointing consolation prizes here for those who are not winners. We are blessed with handsome parting gifts bestowed through the love of a victorious Savior.

John 15:1-8

Branches On The Jesus Tree

In the gospel according to John, Jesus speaks of his identity using a variety of metaphors. He speaks of himself as the bread of heaven, as the light of the world, as the way, the truth and the life. In John 8, as he responds to the challenge of some Pharisees, Jesus seems to speak of his identity by simply saying "I am," echoing God's response to Moses from the burning bush when Moses asks for God's name (cf. John 8:58, Exodus 3:14). In the upper room with his disciples, Jesus gave them another way of knowing him. He said to them, "I am the true vine, and my Father is the vinegrower" (John 15:1).

I don't know a great deal about grapevines and vineyards, but I learned something about growing fruit while serving as pastor of a church in southern Pennsylvania. Adams County is Pennsylvania's fruit basket. The home where we lived next to the church was surrounded on all sides by orchards. I watched every phase of the annual cycle of fruit growing. I watched trees bear loads of peaches, apples, and cherries — more than I ever imagined could come from one place. I watched autumn's frost take the leaves from the trees, and the winter snow cover up all memory of the harvest. I saw miles upon endless miles of beautiful blossoms in the spring.

For all of that, the trees still seemed rather passive participants in this cycle of life. Sure, it's the trees that bear the fruit, but it seems like the fruit growers are doing the heavy work. Some mornings, while lying in bed, I would hear the tractors towing sprayers into the orchards to spray the trees and protect them from pests and parasites. Some evenings

I would watch them returning from the orchards with their headlights on. The entire day had been spent in spraying.

It takes great care and patience to be a fruit grower. Jesus said, "I am the true vine, and my father is the vinegrower," the gardener, the fruit grower (John 15:1). As I watched the annual cycle of fruit growing in Adams County, I watched the orchard workers out in the late fall and winter pruning trees. I sometimes wondered if having branches lopped off, even dead branches, caused the trees to feel anything like what we call pain. I've had some things removed from my body, cut away, that were causing me to be sick, or that threatened my health. Even though that kind of surgery was necessary for my well-being, it was still painful. It's kind of bizarre to think about someone approaching you with a scalpel because they care about you, but that's the fact of it.

Just as the orchard workers prune away the dead and diseased wood from fruit trees, God prunes us. And sometimes that pruning is painful. Perhaps it has been a relationship that has been detrimental to our growth that has needed to be severed. Maybe we have had to give up some cherished notions of what was right, or good, or proper, because we have been confronted with the word of God in such a way that we were brought to confess that those cherished notions were wrong. The word of God can bring us comfort and sustain us at times when we have been brought low and broken by the hardness of life, but that same word can also confront us with our own falsehood, purge and prune from us our unholy relationships, and our unholy convictions. When God confronts us in this way with the Word, it is always with love, always with the certainty that what God takes away, God takes away for the sake of our wholeness and wellbeing. Yet, that kind of pruning can still be painful.

I watched the orchard workers prune the trees, but I also saw something more radical than pruning. I watched bulldozers push out entire rows of trees and cast them into a fire because they carried something called plum pox virus. I can only guess about whether or not those uprooted trees felt any kind of pain, but I know the fruit growers felt the pain of those lost trees. It was more than just the pain of lost potential fruit and income; it was the pain of years of labor, care, of early morning spraying and late winter pruning lost. Nevertheless, the trees had to come out. They had to be burned so that the fruit of the healthy trees might not be corrupted and lost, too. And the image of God as the vine grower, the fruit grower, is no less appropriate in this scenario. In God's orchard there will be trees lost, in spite of all the care and nurture that can be given. No one feels the pain of that loss more acutely than the fruit grower.

Fruit never hangs from the trunk of the tree; it only grows on the branches. It's the branches of the tree that bear fruit, but I've never seen a branch bring forth any apples or peaches after it was cut from the tree. Inasmuch as it's the branch that must remain strong and green and bear the fruit, there is little it can do for itself with regard to fruit bearing beyond remaining firmly fixed in the tree. It's only from the tree that a branch can draw the water and nutrients it needs to bear fruit, albeit with the loving care of the fruit grower.

We show the world our place with Jesus as we bear the fruit of faithful witness to his love for us, testifying to his grace, and living lives of service. However, there is little we can do for ourselves in this calling, this vocation of bearing fruit, beyond remaining firmly fixed and abiding in him. It is only from his life that we draw strength and grace needed to bear the God-glorifying fruit of love as branches on the Jesus tree.

John 16:12-15

Eggshells, Yolks, And Whites

I had a friend in college who was a real math wizard. I've always held in awe people who major in mathematics, because I've always been mathematically challenged. I struggle to balance a checkbook, let alone do all kinds of algorithms and complex equations with numbers to the nth power.

My college friend wasn't a Christian. I don't think he practiced any religion, really. He wasn't a militant atheist, but he was a person my patron saint, John Wesley, might have talked about as someone insensible of his spiritual peril. Despite my efforts of witnessing to Matt, he wasn't responsive. However, he would banter with me good naturedly on matters of faith and I would banter with him about what I found abstract in math.

"How can you work with negative numbers?" I would prod him. "How can there be something that represents a value less than nothing? You can't have less than nothing!"

He would in turn prod me by saying something like "How can you talk about Father, Son, and Holy Spirit and then say you worship one God and not three gods?"

I felt he had a point because I know a lot of Christians, as well as non-Christians, who feel talk about the Trinity is more confusing than it's worth. It's something eggheads in divinity school quibble over, but hardly a matter of practical importance to the average Christian. Jesus didn't seem to make a big deal of it, so why should we? Yet our belief that we worship one God known in three persons has been a central belief of the church throughout the centuries.

We don't read in the gospels of Jesus using the word Trinity, but he does speak of himself in relation to his Father in heaven and to the Holy Spirit. Especially in the gospel according to John, Jesus emphasizes that he doesn't speak on his own, that what he taught is not something of human invention, but that everything originated with God his Father. In the reading today, Jesus assures his disciples that the Advocate whom Jesus promises, the Holy Spirit, will not speak on his own but will continue among them the ministry of God's word that was initiated in Jesus. Jesus and the Father and the Holy Spirit are all of one mind, of one will, and they share one vision. They are one, even though they come to us in three persons.

Still, it's difficult for us to get our minds and hearts around all of this. Sometimes in trying to teach about the Trinity, especially to young people in confirmation classes, I think at times I've done more harm than good. Pastors are always looking for some concrete illustration to use, and we've come up with some dillies to illustrate the Trinity to confirmation classes. For example, there's the illustration using an egg. An egg has a yolk, and the white, and of course the eggshell. They are each distinct, but all part of one egg.

The problem with illustrations like the egg is that they all break down somewhere. Yolk, white, and shell are all part of one egg, but they don't interpenetrate each other unless you throw the egg against the wall! I thought about doing that here to prove my point, but I know the janitor wouldn't appreciate it.

Our profession of one God in three persons, Father, Son, and Holy Spirit, must be important if we go to such great lengths to teach about it, defend it in witnessing to non-Christians, and take a Sunday out of the year to celebrate as Trinity Sunday. It isn't just a mental exercise for divinity school professors or some ancient idea in the church that isn't relevant anymore. Believing in one God as three persons has real, practical importance for living the Christian faith.

Maybe it would help if we moved away from some of those confirmation class illustrations and thought about the Father, Son, and Holy Spirit as a community — the community of God. We say God is eternal. Human community comes and goes. Years ago, I had reason to drive through the Pennsylvania coal mining town of Centralia on a regular basis. Centralia is the place where a mine fire beneath the town caused the place to become uninhabitable. Every time I would drive through the town, I would see that another house had been boarded shut or another building torn down. Eventually, Centralia disappeared and even the roadway through the town was rerouted away from the area. Human community, no matter how strong, comes and goes.

The community that is God — Father, Son, and Holy Spirit — has always been and will always be. Even the Son of God, coming to earth and taking on human nature and human flesh, dying as a human being and passing into death didn't change that. The love and power of God, the community of the Father, Son and Holy Spirit, was not diminished in its power and love. It is everlasting.

We Christians say that God is known as Trinity, God in three persons, the community of the Father, Son, and Holy Spirit. We also confess that human beings are made in the image of God. If we believe we are created in God's image, this understanding of God in a community of three persons has some real implications for how we live. Since God is known as a community that means that we human beings are created for community. We can't live as authentic Christians outside of community. There is no such thing as a solitary Christian.

This community that we are part of is called church. The church is a community bonded in oneness through its profession of Jesus as Lord — not a profession made just with our mouths, but with how we spend our money, how we use our time, and how we treat one another.

I grew up in a congregation whose greatest attribute seemed to be its tendency for members to squabble with one another. My pastor used to say, tongue-in-cheek, "See how these Christians love one another." He was scolding us that we really weren't living in the image of God, where the Father, Son, and Holy Spirit are bound together in love and common life. We are made in the image of God, so we are made for life in community — community that lives bound by mutual love and by our profession of the Lordship of Jesus.

Another thing we say about this God known in three persons is that no one person of the Trinity is subordinate to another. The Father is truly and fully God, the Son is truly and fully God, and the Holy Spirit is truly and fully God. So the church, the community of Christian disciples created in God's image, doesn't recognize any subordination of people, either. This is what Paul the apostle wanted the Galatians to recognize when he wrote to them, saying, "There is no longer Jew or Greek, there is no longer slave or free, there is no longer male and female; for all of you are one in Christ Jesus" (Galatians 3:28).

So there is no hierarchy of persons in the Trinity, and there is no hierarchy of people in the church. We do say that certain people have been set aside for particular ministries. Pastors are folks called of God, gifted of the Holy Spirit for pastoral ministry, and ordained to lives of word, order, sacrament, and service in the church. But that doesn't make them on a higher plane somehow than any other people in the church. Bishops are consecrated to be leaders and teachers of the whole church, but they are not on a higher plane than other persons in the church. Just as there are no subordinates in the Trinity, we are not to see someone as holier than another by virtue of church office; we are all called to be the holy people of God, with some called to perform certain ministries for the sake of the church's life and order.

I think this has some implications for us as church living in the world. The church is a particular community living as a reflection of God through its unity in professing Jesus as Lord. But we also share in community with all people everywhere, because we say that all people are made in the image of God. We have a responsibility to treat others, Christian or non-Christian, with a love that acknowledges relationship without any subordination of one person to another. So while we ought to be known as Christians by our love for each other, we also are called to love all people as being made in God's image.

You know, when the powers of the world want to convince us that we ought to keep certain groups behind walls, or that basic needs ought to be provided to some people before others, that contradicts our profession of faith in the Trinity. We say that all people in the community of the Trinity are equally God, and that we are made in God's image. So when we agree to recognize some people as privileged, especially regarding the basic needs of life, we deny the faith we profess.

There is one other aspect of our belief in one God in three persons very relevant to our living out our discipleship. We say that the second person of the Trinity, God the Son, has come among us as human. He has become incarnate, we say, taken on our human nature. Jesus Christ didn't do this for thirty-odd years on earth, and then shuck our humanity like a worn out suit when he was resurrected and ascended. Jesus Christ has taken on our human nature forever. That community of God in three persons includes our humanity because of what Jesus, the Son of God, has done.

Before the Son of God became incarnate, a great divide separated us from God. God was three persons, but exclusively divine, completely different from finite, sinful humanity. But since God the Son took on human nature, was crucified, dead, and buried, on the third day rose again and ascended to the Father, that great divide has been bridged forever. Humanity, utterly unlike God, has been included within the community of God, Father, Son, and Holy Spirit.

If the Father, Son, and Holy Spirit have, out of love, included us humans—completely different from God—aren't we called to do the same thing, include in our community, out of love, those different from ourselves? It's been said that the most segregated time in America is Sunday morning. Maybe it's beneficial for Christians of different languages and cultural expressions to be able to worship in their native language and celebrate God through their unique traditions. But if that is so, we also need to be about exploring how we can be in unity with Christians different in race, language, and ethnic background from ourselves through joint missions, combined outreach, and gathering with one another frequently in Christian conferencing. We need to explore more intentionally how we can live in this way in the image of the Trinity.

The fumbling efforts to explain God as Trinity using an egg, or whatever thing, probably miss the mark and do cause a giggle here or there. We need to exercise some humility about what we think can really explain about God. But in the Gospels, Jesus makes pretty clear his relation to God the Father and the Holy Spirit. And Jesus' relationship with us makes our belief in God as a community of three persons pretty relevant to our discipleship. The bottom line is that the best illustration we have for the Trinity should be right here: you and I and all of us living, worshiping, and witnessing together in the community called church. Let us pray:

God in three persons, Father, Son, and Holy Spirit: empower us and inspire us to live more faithfully in your image. Convict us when we deny our profession. Grant us grace for repentance. Strengthen us as to live in unity with one another, loving the world for which you became human, died and rose again, and welcoming into the community of the church that great diversity of your children. Amen.

John 17:1-26

How Do You Know?

I am a big fan of British comedy. I enjoy *Are You Being Served?*, *The Last of the Summer Wine*, *Blackadder*, *Mr. Bean*, and, along with many of my generation, *The Flying Circus*. But, my favorite British comedy is that creation of John Cleese and Connie Booth entitled, *Fawlty Towers*.

Named the number one television program of all time by the British Film Institute, *Fawlty Towers* features John Cleese as Basil Fawlty, a much put-upon manager of a seaside hotel in Torquay. Prunella Scales plays Sybil Fawlty, Basil's domineering wife. My favorite recurring scene from *Fawlty Towers* is Sybil talking on the phone to a troubled family friend. Over and over again, Sybil says with exaggerated affect, "I knooow, Oh, I knooow!"

Sybil's over-dramatically sympathizing responses are a source of great laughter. The viewer never really knows what Sybil is talking about, but we are sure her "I knooow!" is simply insincere agreeableness. We laugh, not only because of the comic value of her affect, but because we know that her exaggerated language betrays Sybil's complete lack of knowing the troubles of her conversation partner.

We laugh at Sybil because we see something of ourselves in her emotion-laden insincerity. We know we don't know what we claim we know, and our bold claims of knowing hide our nervous ignorance. Sometimes our attempts at hiding ignorance are harmless and laughable. However, if when asked about our knowledge of God and of Jesus Christ, we deflect or offer agreeable but vague statements of humility, we may in fact be hiding a serious and dangerous spiritual void.

"And this is eternal life, that they may know you, the only true God, and Jesus Christ whom you have sent" (John 17:3). This definition of eternal life that we hear Jesus give in our gospel reading can make us want to stick our hands in our pockets and stare at our shoes. What does it mean to know God in such a way that we can call it eternal life? How can we engage this kind of knowing?

A whole philosophy of how we know what we know exists. It is called "epistemology," which simply means "the study of knowing." Philosophers specializing in epistemology talk of three kinds of knowledge. The first is propositional knowledge, or "knowing that." A simple statement of propositional knowledge might be "I know that $2 + 2 = 4$." That is simple propositional knowledge.

Some religious belief is no more profound than propositional knowledge. "I know that there is a God," is a simple statement of propositional knowledge. The New Testament Letter of James parodies such belief. "Show me your faith apart from your works, and by my works will show you my faith," writes James. Then he continues, "You believe that God is one; you do well. Even the demons believe — and shudder" (James 2:18b-19). So it doesn't seem that propositional knowledge, "knowing that" is knowledge of God that equates to eternal life.

A second kind of knowing talked about by philosophers of epistemology is called procedural knowledge, or "knowing how." You can have propositional knowledge of a subject without having "know-how." For instance, I can tell you I know that if you drive a motorcycle through a 33-foot-radius steady-state turn at 22 mph you must lean into the turn at an angel of 45.6 degrees. I know that through the law of circular motion. But I can tell you that I don't know how to actually perform that turn on a motorcycle. I don't ride!

A lot of Christian faith today, it seems, is hung up on what we might call "faith by procedural knowledge." How can I know the will of God? That's a very popular question in Christian spiritual formation today. How can I have a deeper devotional life? How can I pray? Whole books are written about prayer method. There is centering prayer, meditation, contemplative prayer, *lectio divina* — or praying the scriptures. Prayer position is often discussed in books, with an understanding that one can remain better focused and avoid a wandering mind if one assumes the right posture in prayer. I remember getting a good chuckle from an Anglican priest of a past generation, named Urban T. Holmes III, who made light of the prayer-posture issue by claiming that Anglicans typically prayed in the "shampoo position," which he described as head bowed with one's hands on the forehead and fingers interlaced, as if keeping the lather out of your eyes while getting your hair washed![6] I think you can gather from my explication of "faith by procedural knowledge," that this is not knowing God in the way Jesus was talking about.

But, there is a third kind of knowledge that philosophers identify but are typically reticent to discuss. It is called "acquaintance knowledge." I think that term is somewhat inadequate. Acquaintance knowledge is the knowledge of personal encounter, of engagement with, the object of knowledge. I think "intimacy knowledge" might be a better term. When we use that euphemism about knowing someone in the "biblical sense," as in the King James Bible stating that "Adam knew Eve his wife; and she conceived" (Genesis 4:1), we are talking about this kind of knowledge. Perhaps that sounds a bit too bold, too sensual, even. But I think when we read Jesus saying, "And this is eternal life, that they may know you, the only true God, and Jesus Christ whom you have sent," this is the kind of knowing that Jesus is talking about.

---

6   See Urban T. Holmes, *Spirituality for Ministry* (San Francisco: Harper & Row, 1982).

Eternal life is knowing God intimately, and Jesus Christ whom God has sent. It is a relationship that is deep, interpenetrating, and spiritually intimate. This is a knowing-in-relationship that makes the question, "how can I know the will of God?" redundant and absurd. This is a relationship worth all of one's effort. It is the only knowledge worth giving one's self to utterly and completely. This being said, there does remain a question of how. How does one enter into this kind of communion with God?

Of course, the quick-and-dirty answer is "prayer." And from there we can easily be led back into a cycle of "faith by procedural knowledge," and get caught in an endless round of reading manuals on prayer. But let's take a little different tack on the question of how we enter into intimate communion with God. It remains a how-to question, but let's not focus too much on method. Instead of thinking about a method of prayer, let's think in terms of an approach to prayer as the beginning of intimate communion with God. I believe a real model for an authentic approach to prayer communion with God is to be found in Jesus' prayer in John 17.

In this passage often referred to as Jesus' "high priestly prayer," he begins by talking with God the Father about their relationship. He speaks of the work the Father had given him to do, that he has completed it. He talks of the glory he shared with the Father, and the communion they shared before the world began. Then, Jesus prays for his friends: his disciples. He prays that they may be strengthened for the mission Jesus has handed on to them, of making the Father known. He prays that they may be protected from evil, and that they may not succumb to the pressures of the world. He prays for those who will become disciples in the future, and that they may know the kind of communion with one another and with him and with the Father that those first disciples have known.

How about that? Jesus prays that you and I might have the kind of communion with him and God that Father, that knowing-in-relationship, which is eternal life. Have you ever stopped to ponder that Jesus prays for you that you and he may have an intimate, spiritually interpenetrating relationship? The point is: it doesn't all come down on our shoulders to "know God." Finally, Jesus prays that we may all be together with him to know the glory in love that he has known with the Father.

If we might use this as a model approach for engaging a growing intimacy with God, we are led to a rather provocative beginning in prayer. We are led to begin in prayer by talking about ourselves and about the relationship we desire with God. It's provocative because we tend to believe that God frowns on us focusing on self. That's certainly true when it goes too far, but I think God is keenly interested in each one of us. God loves you — it almost sounds trite, but it's true! I believe God wants you to begin by sharing your frustrations, your dreams, your desires — yourself — in prayerful conversation. Yes, you'll struggle to be honest. Yes, you'll try to hide things from God, foolish as you are. But, if you keep at the conversation, remembering that it is a conversation, which requires your listening for God's word back to you as much as sharing your words with God, you will discover that God uses this conversation to transform your life. In the growing relationship we become more open and honest because we find that this God is trustworthy — we can trust ourselves to God.

You can move forward in the relationship by conversing with God about your concerns for your human intimates: your family, your friends, your closest neighborhoods. You can begin to expand in the relationship to take in others. In fact, you will not be able to avoid it. And as God grows your soul through your increasing intimacy, your growing knowing-in-relationship, you will begin to share with God your concerns for the larger world, the people you don't know or don't know yet, who you know to be as significant to God as you are yourself.

"And this is eternal life, that they may know you, the only true God, and Jesus Christ whom you have sent." Communion with God, intimate knowledge of the Father, knowing Jesus Christ in relationship: this is the "I know" that is eternal life!

John 19:28-30

The Sponge

"I am thirsty." You could see the words form on his lips, but no sound came from his mouth. The woman at his bedside was holding a small cellulose sponge on the end of what looked like a swizzle stick. She dipped it into the foam cup filled with water before swabbing it on the lips and gums of the old man lying in the bed. I thought I heard her sob just a little as she performed this tiny act of kindness, but upon looking back up at her I changed my mind. Perhaps the sound had come from the old man for whom the little bit of moisture the sponge carried may have been enough solace to elicit a soft moan. Her face was drawn with fatigue and sadness, but there was no sign of hot emotion. She had the look of someone in the midst of an ordeal, but also a look of determination bent on seeing the situation through. She was not young, but not nearly as old as the man in the bed. He was her father.

The old man had been lying relatively still since the nurse had come in and administered the morphine sulfate under his tongue. His gray hair was quite thin and wispy. The grimace on his pale face had relaxed a little. His lips were cracked and peeling. His arms, thin and bony, were purple with bruises from the previous injections and blood draws, when his daughter and the doctors thought there still might be a recovery. But that misery was past. Now the only ones about the bed were the pastor and the devoted daughter. There were no more needles and no more prodding, just the foam cup filled with water and the little sponge on the stick.

She sat back in her chair, still holding the foam cup. All that remained was to be present, to respond to any signs of need or finality from the dying man, and to wait. We didn't speak. There was no reason to speak. Most everything of any importance had been said, and words now were superfluous. Our primary source of comfort was no longer words, but the cup of water and the sponge — and it was comfort for all of us. That's how it is when one is nose-to-nose with death. What we had in another time thought so needful, so important, the source of strength or comfort or fortitude is now just so much of life's jetsam. What is significant and essential when we are squared up with mortality is the silent presence, the slight yet loving touch, the small bit of moisture that frees the tongue from cleaving to the roof of one's mouth.

"I am thirsty." What a mundane utterance! The flesh has its needs, even in its final moments, and Jesus acknowledged the crying need of his own human body as he hung between heaven and earth in the hot sun of the Judean afternoon. Words were no longer needed, and everything needing to be said had been said. The comfort Jesus received came in a wine-soaked sponge on the end of stick. It is small comfort, yes, but adequate, because it came from a few devoted friends who stayed nearby even though they were sick themselves with fear and sorrow.

They could do no more than offer the sponge in response to Jesus' final physical need, and so the sponge was comfort to them, too, in the face of their painful helplessness.

How utterly absurd to think we can make a difference in a world of such vast need! It can be overwhelming to go forth in the name of Jesus seeking to minister to the hurting, the homeless, the least, the last, and the lost. To throw all that we have and are into the relief of world poverty or peacemaking or social justice can make us feel like a single freshwater raindrop falling straight into the salty ocean.

A friend of mine is a clinical psychologist who works with war veterans suffering from depression. Once as we talked together, he said to me, "So many of these men tell me that whenever they see stories on the television news of a child abduction, or catastrophes that kill dozens of people, they begin to have suicidal thoughts."

"What do you say in response?" I asked. "What do you counsel them to do?"

"I tell them not to watch those reports," he said. "When they declare that not to watch is cowardly escapism, I tell them it's only escapism when you are confronted with a situation you can change, but you choose to look away. So I encourage them to look for situations where they can become involved and make a difference. Maybe it's reading to first-grade children. Maybe it's calling bingo at the senior center. Those things are small. They seem unimportant, but they are really significant because they make a difference. They contribute."

How much the smallest kindness means! In some mysterious way, such acts of love make a lasting change in the fabric of the universe. They tie together broken threads and make the weave in the whole of all things complete. They are small; when looked at as singular actions they seem to be no more than minutiae. But they contribute to the amount of love in the world. They move the kingdom of God to its fulfillment.

John writes that Jesus' saying, "I am thirsty," was really in order to fulfill some messianic prophecy. Could his mission really not be finished without saying those words? Or, was the response of those nearby who cared for him required as well? Did it somehow take the inclusion of one final, tiny act of loving kindness by the three woman and the beloved disciple to make the work complete? We have only the Evangelist's words to go on, but he seems to communicate that the whole thing was of some necessity. A sponge soaked in sour wine was lifted to those cracked and bleeding lips. And "when he had received the wine, he said, 'It is finished.' Then he bowed his head and gave up his spirit" (John 19:30).

The woman at her father's bedside leaned forward as she again dipped the little cellulose sponge on the stick in her cup. She gently pushed it past the old man's lips and swabbed his tongue and gums. His mouth puckered around the sponge for a moment, sucking the small amount of water from it. As she sat back again, he licked his lips just a bit without opening his eyes. How many hours might yet remain before death did its task, before the old man's life would be finished and he might be relieved of his tether to earth's air, light, and water?

We stepped out of the room as I prepared to leave. As we stood by the door, the daughter looked at me for a moment before speaking, and I held her eye in looking back at her. I was their pastor. I had spent my ministry in this parish preaching to them, but preaching was not the order of this day. Then she spoke what she had yet to say.

"My Dad sat by mother's bedside at home when she died of cancer. The last two days of her life, he didn't leave her side. He did whatever needed done for her. Those last two nights he slept in a chair. He never asked or demanded anything like that from me, but I made a promise to myself that I would do for him, if and when the time came, in that same manner."

I didn't say anything in return just then. I just continued to look her in the eyes. Finally she asked the question that we both knew was on her mind.

"Do you think he knows I'm here? Do you think he knows it's me?"

"I really believe he knows you're by his side," I told her. "But even if he doesn't, you need to be here, doing what you're doing, because it fulfills your word. Besides that," I said to her, "what you are doing here matters. It matters more than you or I may ever know."

John 20:1-18

Searching, Sought After, Found

Have you ever had the frustration of going for that tool you need to do a job, only to discover it's not where it should be? I'm not talking only to carpenters and mechanics. Any cook who has ever misplaced that favorite slotted spoon, or any gardener unable to locate that hand cultivator with the especially comfortable grip, has known this kind of frustration.

I remember when I was growing up that my Dad sometimes discovered he had tools missing, and he would sometimes assume I was the one who had used them and failed to get them back where they belonged. He would call me into the garage and say, "I'm missing such-and-such a tool. It hangs right there." Then he would point to the place on the wall where he always kept such-and-such a tool. I guess that was supposed to remind me that I had taken it and not returned it.

Discovering that something you need is missing can be annoying, but it pales in comparison to the discovery that your child is missing. Perhaps he has gone off somewhere, quietly playing in his secret place. Perhaps your daughter has wandered off from you while shopping in a department store. In that kind of scenario you can experience real, choking panic — especially in an age of the growing horror of child abductions.

It is that kind of panicky fear that Mary Magdalene experienced at the empty tomb on that first Easter morning. The body of Jesus was gone. It was the only remaining vestige of a relationship that had given her life hope, and now even that was taken away from her. She went running back to the only two people left whom she could rely on, and they responded to her news of the disappearance of Jesus' body by rushing immediately to the tomb.

But what did these two men eventually do for Mary? Very little, it seems. After running to the tomb, we can imagine them arriving and acting a bit like ants casing a summer picnic. The beloved disciple arrived first, but he looked tentatively into the tomb and did not go in. He was apparently afraid to enter. Peter, the slower one, arrived and, true to form, crashed in where wise men feared to tread. This seemed to give the beloved disciple courage and he entered the tomb, too. He then saw what Peter saw: the linen wrappings lying there, and the cloth that had been on Jesus' head, not lying with the linen wrappings but rolled up in a place by itself. In verse eight of our passage, the scripture reads that when the beloved disciples saw all of this, he believed. But, believed what? Did he believe that Jesus had been raised, or that his body had been stolen? The only logical conclusion he reached seems to be that Jesus' body was gone, as Mary had said, because the passage continues in verse nine stating that "they did not yet understand the scripture, that he must rise from the dead."

The reaction of Peter and John is amazed stupefaction. They display belief in Mary's report, but hardly what we would call faith or belief in the resurrection. In fact, the two men were so stupefied by what they discovered that they just turned around and went home, insensitively leaving Mary behind to cry outside the tomb. She remained behind: anxious, alone, and grief stricken. Her world was in pieces. The only people she felt she could turn to fail to even try to console her. And then, a most terrifying thing occurred. The scene of grief and despair was interrupted by the appearance of heavenly beings. "Woman, why are you weeping?" they asked her. But Mary's mind was so transfixed on the finality of Jesus' death that even the appearance of angels didn't lead her to suspect a divine intervention. She would only reiterate that the dead body of Jesus had been taken from the tomb. "They have taken my Lord away," she replied to them, "and I do not know where they have laid him."

It is just then that Jesus appeared, not as a corpse, or a ghost, but as the resurrected Lord — and he asked her the same question as the angel. Still, the concrete reality of physical death could not be broken in Mary's mind, despite this appearance of the resurrected Jesus. Only after he spoke her name, directly addressing her as he must have on so many prior occasions, did Mary cry out, "Rabbouni!" in recognition of her teacher and friend, Savior, and Lord.

The story of Mary at the tomb illustrates how difficult it was for first-century Christians to be convinced of something beyond mortality, and of life on a higher plane than we experience on this side of death. They were no more credulous than people today. If it is difficult for many twenty-first century people to accept something as radical as resurrection, it was no less difficult for people in the first century.

We gather on Easter morning to be reminded again of the hope that God's power is not limited by the confines of this material world. We gather to be reassured that there is something more to all of us than this flesh we wear. But can this story of Mary at the tomb do something more than just warm our hearts? Is there more to this gospel account than a touching story of reunion? Can it, in fact, lead us to a deeper faith, a greater confidence in the truth of resurrection for our own lives? I believe it can.

First, this story tells us that an empty tomb proves nothing. Christianity has never ultimately relied upon an empty grave as evidence. The faith of the apostles and early Christians was based, not upon the empty tomb, but upon encounter with the resurrected Jesus. Mary did not believe because Jesus was not in the grave; she was still incredulous. And it was because she sought after a dead Jesus that she could not find him.

If we are content with a dead Jesus — a Jesus who walked and talked and died in Palestine 2,000 years ago, then we will not engage the reality of resurrection life. What Jesus did in teaching and performing his miraculous signs and healings may inspire us. They may fill us with emotion, but they remain history to us unless we have personally encountered the living Christ. Singing "He lives, Christ Jesus lives today," will never get us beyond the sentimentality of a sweet hymn if we have not ourselves confronted the resurrected one.

Perhaps you feel this puts a terrible burden on you to seek and find the Christ for yourself. Perhaps you have already invested much of yourself in going after one spiritual experience after another in search of an encounter with the Living Lord. If so, then stop! Notice that for all of Mary's earnest searching, she did not find Christ. He found her. This is the whole point of John's gospel. We worship a seeking God who is not dissuaded from his pursuit of us. Among the very first words of God to humanity we read in the Bible are the words called out to Adam in Genesis 2 after the fall: "Where are you?"

Jesus told the parable of the lost coin to emphasize God's relentless pursuit of us. In that parable you have one lost piece of silver, unable to cry out, unable to come back on its own. The coin's owner sweeps the entire house until that coin is retrieved, and then she rejoices in its recovery. Don't drive yourself mad in the pursuit of that next spiritual experience in the hope of encountering Jesus. Even when we are so badly lost that we cannot even cry out, Jesus is seeking us. Even when we don't want to be found, he is searching for us. If you seem to have lost Christ, if your spiritual life has dimmed and become thin, and drab, and meager, you can be sure that he is searching for you, that he will not let you go, and that he yearns for you. Like the owner of the lost coin, he seeks diligently until he finds.

There's one more thing from this story we need to allow to reassure us. Mary didn't recognize the Lord at first, even after she encountered him. That's not terribly unusual. The two who encountered the risen Christ on the road to Emmaus did not recognize him at first, either. The testimony of many of the saints through the ages has been that they did not immediately identify the Risen Christ when they encountered him. Take Saint Francis, for instance.

It's written that Francis was terrified of lepers and leprosy. One day, while walking down a narrow road, he saw the horribly white, disfigured form of a leper coming toward him. His mind began to race, his heart pounded. He sought some way to avoid the encounter with this leper, but there was nowhere to go. Fear overtook Francis, and then shame. In response to those feelings of shame, Francis mustered his courage and ran toward the leper. He threw his arms about him as they met, embraced him, and kissed him, and then went on. Francis only made a few steps before turning around and looking back after the leper, but he was gone. There was nothing behind him but the empty road.

So often we do not recognize the risen Christ, at first. He is masked to us, cloaked in the form of a despondent brother or sister, a needy neighbor, a suffering child or a lonely elder. But when we risk the encounter, we discover ourselves in the presence of the living God — in the company of the Risen Christ. And it is in that encounter, in that presence, that we experience a foretaste and an assurance of our own resurrection.

John 20:1-18

It Happened In A Garden

It happened in a garden,
That tragedy of all tragedies,
Was it in the steaminess of mid-morning
The idea first came to bud and blossom?
Did it take long for a serpent's subtle seed to germinate?
How fertile is the human mind!
How damp and warm it is
In the dark recesses of the consciousness,
Where analysis gently waters thinking,
And thus sprout schemes and plots.

"Did Yahweh say, 'eat not of any fruit'?" he asked.
The broadness of the question seems quite calculated.
Recalling the vast bounty of all that offers life
Makes even more conspicuous and strangely tempting
The single forbidden, deadly thing.

"Eat any, save this one," she answered in her innocence.
Yet even then her thought was being furrowed,
The lush green sod of her heart purity turned over by the
question.
"To do so is to die," she went on,
But her voice now lacked a certain certainty.
"You will not die," he firmly spoke to her
With all the conviction she had lost
("At least not right away," he hissed only to himself).
"This fruit expands the mind,
Gives one cosmic consciousness," he declared.
"Puts one on par with God."

How tempting the gift of the expanded mind,
The cosmic consciousness, to those most spiritually ambitious!
The same was the later promise of lysergic diethylamide —
LSD to most and just acid to the rest.
But how much stretching will the limited human mind withstand?
How much cosmic consciousness will fit into a jar of clay
Before it shatters into fragments
And the soul is blown into metaphysical dust?
Ah — there's the rub!
Despite our cold calculating, we've never been able to know
How little is too much.
Why should the woman bear blame for that trait common to us all?

"Take, eat," implored the legless one.
Or was it the voice in her head she heard?
No matter. How pretty!
How desirable, despite the danger.
And so partake she did, and with her partner, too.
And it blew their minds.

It happened in a garden,
In the cool of the day, or so the story goes.
They were apprehended, the evidence overwhelming.
The alterations were obvious —
They were clothed but not in their right minds, really.
The knowledge they had coveted
Looked more like paranoia.

"Where are you?" Yahweh called in brokenhearted grief.
"Hidden," came their answer, "clothed only by leaves of fig
And our fear of Thee."

No more was it a garden.
No more did life rise freely from the earth.
Now it must be coaxed from thorns and thistles by his sweat.
So, too, his offspring, which she now would bear in pain.
And when wearied beyond refreshment,
They would rest in the dust from which their bodies came.
And there was death.

It happened in a garden.
They laid his bloody, punctured body down,
Not in mid-morning's heat, nor the cool of the day,
But in the depth of dark, cold night.
The Jewish Day of Preparation.
They sacrificed their place at the festal meal.
Touching a corpse made one unclean,
Unfit for Sabbath solemnities.
Joseph and Nicodemus, these two Pharisees
Reverently wrapped the body.
One hundred pounds of sweet perfume signed their love,
In like manner to Mary's pure nard anointing
Only days before.
Thankfully, the tomb lay close to hand.
To take the body a distance on the Sabbath
Would only compound their grief and guilt;
Layer insult upon injury.

How had it so frightfully come to this?
What drove men to stomp down such truth and beauty?
Such fruitfulness of human soul overflowing with divine
fecundity —
Snuffed out.
What brought it to pass, really?
Was it not the same old deadly seed
That sprouted in the fertile, deep-yet-deadly reaches of hu-
man consciousness
And bore fear when fully ripe?

Yes, familiar paranoia that favors death to life.
He might be competition to Herod, or to Caesar.
Better that he die.
And so, the great round stone sealed the deal, the tomb,
So it was thought.

It happened in a garden.
But then, once again: a woman.
Still was it dark at her arrival, but not deeply so.
In her dim illumination she saw the stone,
Rolled back!
Was he plucked from the resting place of all spent human
clay?
But why?

Off she ran to tell the others, the men,
So that they, too, might partake a glimpse of the empty
tomb.
As she had run to them so they now ran with her in return,
But looking in they spied no spiced body.
It was gone.
Only the remains of the love gift of two Pharisees was found.
And the one who went inside believed —
But what?

So off they went back home,
Once more leaving the woman holding the bag.
She stood and wept, grieved it all —
Lost innocence, lost purity, lost love, lost hope, lost life.
Then a word, a question,
Once more in a garden:
"Why are you weeping?"
Was it asked by another, or had she heard it in her head?

"Because he is lost — altogether lost! —
And I do not know where now he lies!"

And again the question: "Why are you weeping?"
But now, with different voice, from another there,
Unmistakably there.
Perhaps he is the one given to tend the garden,
Yes, truly, he is one with the first garden's gardener —
But more!

He is the One through whom all flowers bloom,
All seeds of goodness, truth, and beauty sprout.
In his body he bore all the ancient antipathies,
The past paranoia and human fears of God's nearer presence.
Reconciled in this One, once wrapped in death,
Are God and humankind.
No dust, no earth, no stone-cold tomb
Could hold such life: the Spirit.

And thus, this One now with woman speaks and speaks her name:
"Mary."
And she with joy, in her native tongue, replies: "Rabbouni!"
And there is life!
It happened in a garden.

We, each one, receive a little plot
To make of it what we will.
Death or life in that small patch
Still hinge upon our choices.
Whose words will we choose to hear?
Whose questions will we heed?
Whose "take, eat" command will we obey —
The serpent's, or the Savior's?
One will take us deeper into thorns and thistles.
The other leads us back into the lushness of a garden,
There to stroll with God
In the cool part of the day.

John 20:1-18

Easter Sunday

"When it rains, it pours." Sometimes problems pile up on top of one another. Our lives seem to be frustrated at every turn. As the first day of the week dawned following that dark Friday afternoon on which Jesus had been crucified, it is certain that the despair of his followers in the face of their shattered hopes was deepening.

At least Jesus' body had received a decent burial, although there had been no funeral and no time for the customary mourning rituals. Now, Mary Magdalene needed fully to mourn his passing. In her sorrow she made her way to the tomb on that bleak Sunday morning. She would still offer her love to him in tears of grief. But upon her arrival at the tomb, not all is as it should be. The stone sealing the tomb's entrance, weighing perhaps two tons, has been rolled back.

Is this how it is to be? Is even his dead body bound to be abused, desecrated, removed from its final resting place? Is even her grieving to be frustrated? Is Good Friday all there is — this abrupt, violent ending?

Maybe you are here today because you are here most Sundays. Maybe you are here today because it's Easter. Maybe you are here today because your hopes and dreams have been dashed, shattered. Your life has been frustrated, and even your attempts to respond to your frustration have been frustrated. You feel like you are in a dead end. Life has become an obstacle too large to overcome.

One year, after an uplifted Palm Sunday time of worship in the church where I was then pastoring, I went home to find the message on my answering machine that my mother had been taken by ambulance to the hospital. She had been experiencing chest pain. My wife and I drove to the emergency room at the hospital where my mom had been taken. We found her hooked to an IV and a heart monitor. Her breathing was difficult, and she was still having pain. More than that, she had become frustrated with her life.

She looked at me from the bed with a mix of anger and pain. "I haven't been good for a year," she said to me. "I have no energy. I keep doctoring, and I get no better. I've been thinking, 'I'm 72 years old. I've lived long enough, and I've lived like this long enough, I can't even seem to die!"

Mary Magdalene, discovering the empty tomb, ran back to tell Simon Peter and another disciple what she had found. Quickly, the two set off to see what had happened. Arriving at the tomb, they discover the stone rolled back just as Mary had said. Simon Peter immediately entered the tomb to discover only disheveled grave clothes. The body of Jesus was gone. It seems that when the evangelist wrote that the other disciple went into the tomb, "and saw and believed," what he believed was Mary's story. They — whoever they were — took the Lord out of the tomb. There's nothing one can do but go home. And the two male disciples did just that. They left Mary alone at the tomb, frustrated and weeping. Everyone was at a loss.

We know about loss. We know that as much as we sometimes try to turn life into a game of gaining all we can, we are losing moment by moment. Studies have shown that with the invention of every labor saving device we have somehow lost discretionary time from our lives. As we grow older, we accumulate things but lose our vitality. We get the big house, but lose the ability to get up and down the stairs. As much as we want to believe we are gaining, we are always losing.

My mother had a heart catheterization the Monday following Palm Sunday. She had heart procedures twice in the past to correct coronary artery blockage. She had in mind that she would receive the same kind of non-invasive procedure used before to help her this time. She might have to do a day in the hospital, followed by some outpatient cardiac rehabilitation.

When I went into the cardiac procedure area after her catheterization, and saw her cardiologist standing beside her bed and holding her hand, I knew things weren't going as hoped.

"Your mother is no longer a candidate for the non-invasive angioplasty procedure," he told me. "She needs open-heart arterial by-pass surgery."

In life, there are losses, and they mean the end of something for us. Things we used to do are no longer possible for our bodies. We encounter impasses that turn us away from familiar ways of living and being. But what looks like an ending when viewed through Easter faith is always a beginning. Easter is about overcoming obstacles. Easter is about loss that becomes miraculous gift, death that issues in new life.

As Mary Magdalene stood weeping outside the tomb, she was confronted by one whom she first mistook for the gardener. She would not perceive that this was the risen Jesus. Resurrection does not come easily to us. New life does not leap down upon us directly from the cross; it emerges from a tomb in the half-light of early morning after a sabbath's rest, so alien to our rutted ways of thinking about reality as to be completely unrecognizable to our hearts and minds. We altogether shun the idea of new life, of resurrection, except when it becomes specific, when it somehow lays a claim upon us personally and calls us out by name. So it was with Mary Magdalene.

When the risen Jesus called out her name, confronted her personally, she acknowledged with joy a reality of life previously beyond the bounds of her acceptance. And her encounter with the resurrected Christ was real enough that she did not merely hold the experience in her heart as some special, private vision. She shared it as public reality, and returned to the community of disciples with a pronouncement: "I have seen the Lord!"

My mother had surgery on Wednesday before Easter: triple by-pass surgery. She came through it well. She wasn't terribly recognizable to me in the recovery room. She looked older, smaller — more wires, tubes, and medical technology than human being. But it was my mother in that bed. Later, she would grow into the reality of renewed life with a repaired heart.

There was no guarantee she would emerge from the operating room as she did. I am not about to tell you that my father, brother, sisters, and I were indifferent to the outcome — that we had reconciled ourselves to the knowledge that Mom would be in a better place, live or die. We share that faith, yes, but we were not daring it to be proven on that Wednesday afternoon. However, I was struck by the unusual calm with which my mother faced her surgery. Always somewhat of a nervous person, she exhibited a peace I had not seen in her before. I noted to her on the morning of her surgery how calm she seemed.

"I'm not going to feel sick anymore," she said to me. "I'm having the surgery. I want to wake up among all of you with a repaired heart, but if I don't, I know I will wake up with God."

It was right then, I believe, that new life called my mother by name.

John 20:19-31

Life After Death

In a psychology of religion course I took in college, the professor spent one class period discussing John 20:19-31. He began the class by passing out photocopies of the text, and then reading the passage aloud while the class followed along. When he finished, he simply asked the class an open discussion question: What's this biblical passage all about?

There were a number of psychology majors in the class along with pre-ministerial students, since this was a church-related liberal arts college. Interspersed among these two dominant groups were some English majors, philosophy majors, and probably some undeclared folks just looking to fulfill a distribution requirement. The responses were as varied as the class make-up.

Some of the psychology majors began to talk about the disciples experiencing delusions of Jesus' appearance among them as the result of group neuroses, wish-fulfillment, or perhaps separation anxiety and fear of the authorities. Pre-ministerial students, some who had actually already seen a biblical commentary and knew how to use it, piped up and went on about Thomas as both a positive and negative example of faith, John's gospel as heavily dependent upon the meaning of signs, and the evangelist's alternative story of the giving of the Holy Spirit to the disciples and the birth of the church. Some English majors, with support from the philosophy contingent, wanted to talk about the use of metaphor in ancient literature and the failure of the church to fully employ literary criticism as an interpretive tool for reading the Bible.

After allowing things to go on for some time, the professor interrupted and asked if anyone thought the passage had anything to say about what happens after you die. Everyone —including, sadly enough, the pre-ministerial students — just looked at each other in silence. The professor went on to register his surprise and disappointment that the entire class had focused their attention on everyone else in the story except Jesus, whose appearance behind locked doors after dying horribly and being buried is the most psychologically, spiritually, and textually provocative thing in the whole passage! He went on to say that he also found it psychologically provocative that everyone in the class avoided the idea that this story was about life after death.

So what does this passage from John's gospel have to say about human existence beyond death? Christianity has historically taught that Jesus Christ opens the way to eternal life for those who place their trust in him. That perhaps raises the question of what trust in Jesus means, which has had a number of interpretations through history. However, the early church maintained the New Testament witness to faith in Jesus as the new Adam, the first-born of the New Creation, whose resurrection from the dead is prototypical for those baptized in his name and thus baptized into his death.

Roman Catholic theologian, Hans Kung, who was eventually excommunicated, was once asked in an interview what a photographer might have been able to capture on film in the upper room on that first Easter evening. Kung answered that there was nothing to photograph, for the resurrection story is simply a poetic way of saying that the work and spirit of Jesus continued on in among the disciple community after his death. In commenting upon Kung's response, conservative Protestant biblical scholar Paul Willoughby wrote that, had photography been available in the first century, a man with a camera would have been able to capture the greatest snapshot in history.[7]

7   Willoughby, 375.

The problem with both the response of Kung and Willoughby is that each assumes empirically verifiable physical existence as the basis upon which to judge the truth of the resurrection. The gospel of John makes clear that, while the resurrected Jesus is the same person who was crucified and that he was recognized as such by his disciples, his presence among them was not physical in the way we typically understand it.

So the most basic Christian understanding of resurrection is that it is spiritual, not physical. This is what Paul the apostle taught in writing to the Corinthians. When addressing the question about how the dead are raised and in what manner of body they come, Paul writes, "It is sown (buried) a physical body, it is raised a spiritual body. If there is a physical body, there is also a spiritual body" (1 Corinthians 15:44).

Thus, "although the doors were shut, Jesus came and stood among them and said, 'Peace be with you'" (John 20:26). Jesus is alive beyond death. He is bodily raised, but he is not flesh and blood as we understand those physical elements. He communicates with those whom he was in relationship during his flesh-and-blood existence.

Going further, the resurrected Jesus is recognizable to his disciples. This is the testimony of the gospel in mentioning that the resurrected Jesus displays his crucifixion scars—not once only, but twice. He first shows the disciples minus Thomas on Easter evening, and then a week later again shows the marks to Thomas in order to evoke the troubled disciple's faith. That the evangelist includes in his account that Jesus twice appeared behind locked doors and twice revealed the scars of his crucifixion signifies the importance of these elements in the story. It emphasizes that the resurrected Jesus is the crucified one, and that his raised body, while sharing continuity with his physical existence, is not the same as his crucified flesh and blood.

Likewise to be noted for its repetition is Jesus' greeting to his disciples: "Peace be with you." It is the simple Middle Eastern greeting as common today as in the first century. But it's repetition as the raised Jesus' greeting to his fearful disciples in the upper room gives it extra meaning. All past betrayals, all past failures, all past hurts have been put aside. This is an assurance of reconciliation and forgiveness: the healing that resurrection offers. Any brokenness of relationship that existed prior to death is now erased, for the new creation exemplified in resurrected life makes all things new.

This is the great paradox of Christian teaching about life after death that finds its grounding in the resurrection of Jesus. After death, you have ongoing communion with those whom you have been in relationship in this life, yet this communion is made new through the healing of past hurts and brokenness. Your relationships are not ultimately broken by death. You are essentially the same person beyond death as before. Yet you are not living any longer in a broken physical body and grieving brokenness in your relationships. You are the same person, but healed, alive in a spiritual body unencumbered by physical limitations and in reconciled, spiritual communion with those whom you loved.

Beyond the doorway of dying we are not a resuscitated corpse, but neither are we a metaphor — alive to our surviving loved ones only through some wispy reminder in the evening breeze or the falling leaves of autumn. If that's all the more I thought resurrection amounted to for Jesus, or for any of us who follow him, I would surrender my ordination credentials and take up some other vocation. At the end of Chapter 20, John the Evangelist told us he had written "so that you may come to believe that Jesus is the Messiah, the Son of God, and that through believing you may have life in his name" (John 20:31). Life in his name is life in the new creation. So may it be.

John 21:1-14

Himself

When everything is said and done,
What is left to say or do?
When the best has seemed to pass,
And inspiration's
Lift has gone flat,
What then?

Sitting and waiting for the end
Is really not an option.
Stories of the glory days
Grow old in telling
Without a sequel.
What now?

We cast about in the darkness,
Hoping for that special catch —
New purpose and direction.
The best is past now.
What was the meaning?
Where to?

This, too, was Peter's dilemma.
Jesus, crucified and raised.
Upper room appearances —
Locked doors? No problems!
Easter!

Ah, but now these days come after.
Mountain top experiences
Lead back into the valley.

The same old world:
Death and taxes.
Go fish.

That's what Peter did. All night long,
Casting nets into the darkness.
Just like back in the old days:
Simon and six friends.
The catch was paltry,
Nothing.

Isn't that how it feels to us?
Bobbing about in the dark,
We just go through the motions.
Prayers are empty words.
Our spirit nets go
Empty.

Worship becomes dreadful duty:
Sitting with people not liked
Doing what doesn't matter.
Our souls become as
Ezekiel's bones:
Too dry.

And the world seems no better.
All efforts fall on deaf ears.
Coarse culture, moral decay,
Gun violence and
Fatherless children.
We're lost.

Is it so good that we've been changed
Yet the world stays the same?
What's the point, to be remade,
Amid the gloom and

Veil of human tears?
Where's hope?

Like Job, sitting in the ashes,
The good times now are all gone.
Yet, we would still press onward
If we could just tell
Which way onward is.
Where to start?

We yearn for old ways, tried and true.
And like them, we go fishing off the
Familiar side of the boat,
Do the same thing and
Hope for new results.
Insane.

But just when they, with aching backs,
Were giving into failure,
Their boats and hearts, both empty,
Then he showed himself
Standing on the shore
Alone.

"You haven't any fish, eh boys?"
"No," they said, not knowing him.
"Try the other side the boat."
The great catch let them
Know that it was him,
The Lord.

And there at seaside they are fed
Breakfast of grilled fish and bread.
Net and stomachs filled, and hearts
Overflowing now
Because there he shows
Himself.

It's true that we have been remade
For works of mercy, justice,
Devotion and for worship.
But we are remade
For more, for love, for
Himself.

We are more than simply servants.
We are not just instruments.
We were made for fellowship.
To be remade his
Friends he gave for us
Himself.

So in our gloom and apathy,
When hearts and backs are aching,
He comes, names our agony,
Calls us by our names
And again he gives
Himself.

No form, no face, we there can see,
But in the dim morning light
We hear his voice and we know
It's him beside us,
And with us, too.
Himself.

He comes, and we draw up the nets,
Run to meet him on the shore.
He bids us, "Come and breakfast,"
And we are fed, renewed,
Because he shows
Himself.

CPSIA information can be obtained
at www.ICGtesting.com
Printed in the USA
BVOW06s1825131117
500307BV00016B/152/P